50 ABSOLUTELY PERFECT RECIPES FOR AMERICA'S FAVORITE DESSERTS

POUND CAKE • CHOCOLATE CAKE • ANGEL FOOD CAKE •
NEW YORK CHEESECAKE • GINGERBREAD • BANANA BREAD
CUPCAKES • CHOCOLATE CREAM PIE • CHERRY PIE •
LEMON MERINGUE PIE • APPLE CRISP • PEACH COBBLER •
PEANUT BUTTER COOKIES • CHOCOLATE CHIP COOKIES •
BROWNIES • COCONUT MACAROONS • BLUEBERRY MUFFINS •
BUTTERMILK BISCUITS • POPOVERS • AND MORE!

"The clearly written recipes in this concise volume are the building
blocks of a competent home baker's repertoire. Kitchen common sense is
fused with familiar ingredients to produce downright yummy cakes,
tea breads, muffins, pies, and cookies—ones you *really* like to eat."

—Beth Hensperger,
author of *Beth's Basic Bread Book*

Since retiring as the CEO of a multimillion-dollar wholesale baking
company, MURRAY JAFFE has become a devoted, dedicated, and mildly
obsessed home baker. He lives in the Napa Valley with his wife,
Marjorie, and two very accurate ovens.

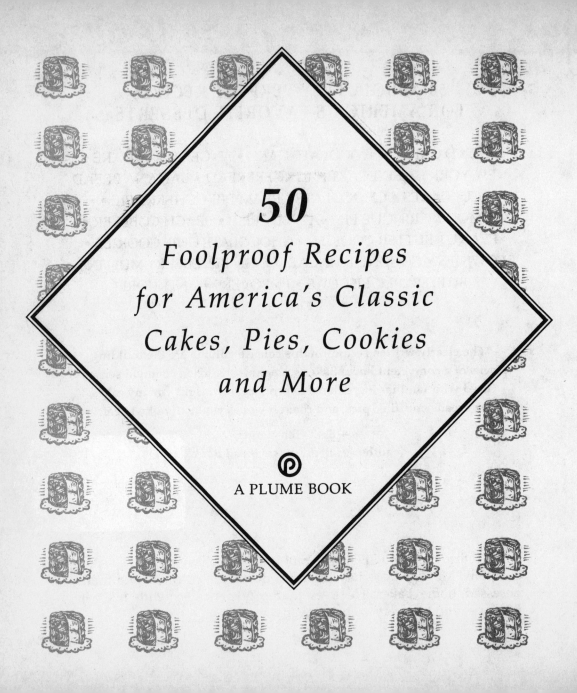

50

*Foolproof Recipes
for America's Classic
Cakes, Pies, Cookies
and More*

Ⓟ

A PLUME BOOK

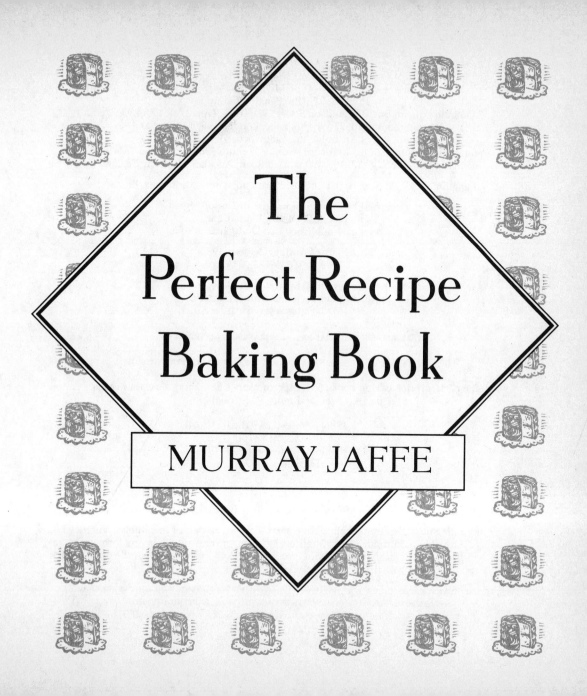

The Perfect Recipe Baking Book

MURRAY JAFFE

PLUME
Published by the Penguin Group
Penguin Putnam Inc., 375 Hudson Street, New York, New York 10014, U.S.A.
Penguin Books Ltd, 27 Wrights Lane, London W8 5TZ, England
Penguin Books Australia Ltd, Ringwood, Victoria, Australia
Penguin Books Canada Ltd, 10 Alcorn Avenue, Toronto, Ontario, Canada M4V 3B2
Penguin Books (N.Z.) Ltd, 182–190 Wairau Road, Auckland 10, New Zealand

Penguin Books Ltd, Registered Offices: Harmondsworth, Middlesex, England

Published by Plume, an imprint of Dutton Signet,
a member of Penguin Putnam Inc.
Previously published in a Dutton edition.

First Plume Printing, October, 1997
10 9 8 7 6 5 4 3 2 1

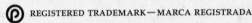 REGISTERED TRADEMARK—MARCA REGISTRADA

The Library of Congress has catalogued the Dutton edition as follows:
Jaffe, Murray.
The perfect recipe baking book : 50 foolproof recipes for America's classic cakes,
pies, cookies, and more / Murray Jaffe.
p.   cm.
ISBN 0-525-94228-9 (hc.)
ISBN 0-452-27749-3 (pbk.)
1. Baking.   2. Desserts.   I. Title.
TX763.J34   1996
641.8'15—dc20   96–21930
CIP

Printed in the United States of America

BOOKS ARE AVAILABLE AT QUANTITY DISCOUNTS WHEN USED TO PROMOTE PRODUCTS OR SERVICES.
FOR INFORMATION PLEASE WRITE TO PREMIUM MARKETING DIVISION,
PENGUIN PUTNAM INC., 375 HUDSON STREET, NEW YORK, NEW YORK 10014.

To
Marjorie Garland Campbell Jaffe
Extraordinary Woman
Extraordinary Companion
Extraordinary Wife

Acknowledgments

My warmest thanks to my wife, Marge, for her patience and good humor while both ovens were continually baking away. Without her intelligent and consistent encouragement, this book would never have seen the light of day.

To my daughter, Barbara Jaffe, who, over many years and in her quiet way, has taught me practically everything I know today about the art and science of baking. Barbara has an uncanny, intuitive grasp of what is right and what is wrong in a recipe and she has managed to impart some of that extraterrestrial knowledge to me. She is a marvelous baker and, if she ever gets around to writing a cookbook, it will be outrageously good.

To my friend and literary agent, Martha Casselman, who saw the future when there was practically nothing to see and who started the wheels moving when they were practically at a standstill. A great person to have on my side.

To my editor, Julia Moskin, who manages to be warm and gracious and still gets exactly what she wants, exactly when she wants it. A rare combination, indeed. I enjoy working with her and feel lucky to have her as my editor.

To my recipe testers, Claudia Jalaty, Anita Reicher, and Rhonda Jemison, for the many hours they so faithfully spent in making sure things turned out the way they were supposed to.

To Brock Palmer, for his great skill at the word processor and for his great interest in everything he was doing.

And finally, my thanks to the good fortune that has landed me here in the beautiful wine country of Napa, California, where the peace, quiet and beauty have made working on this book a joy.

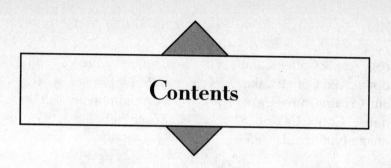

Contents

PIES, CRISPS AND COBBLERS   99

PERFECT PASTRY DOUGH   101

COOKIES AND BROWNIES   153

MUFFINS, BISCUITS AND SCONES   189

FROSTINGS AND GLAZES   209

Index   223

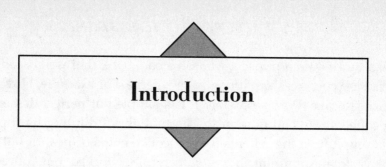

Introduction

The idea for this book came to me one day when I decided to bake a chocolate cake. I turned to my cookbook collection and was faced with a flood of options. Should I use the recipe calling for unsweetened chocolate, unsweetened cocoa or semisweet chocolate? Should I use the one with all-purpose flour or cake flour? White granulated sugar or dark brown sugar? Sweet butter or salted butter or vegetable oil? Should I use recipes calling for baking powder or baking soda or a combination of both, in conjunction with milk or buttermilk or sour cream or boiling hot water or what? I found myself drowning in indecision.

Which was the best recipe? Which one should I use? How could I choose among all of the options without trying them? I found myself wishing that someone had taken the time and trouble to bake them all and then, based on that extensive experience, make the changes and adjustments that were necessary to end up with just one great recipe. I became intrigued with the idea of a baking book that was really simple and completely unintimidating. A book with easy-to-follow, fail-proof recipes. A book that I could use to quickly and easily bake something that was certain to be totally delicious.

Also, since I am a purist, I wanted a cookbook that was based on the classics, not the countless variations on the theme. For example, I love New York–style cheesecake. With a passion! It is a simple but perfect dessert, especially with coffee at the end of a meal. The thought of diluting its superb taste by combining it with ingredients like chocolate chips or peanut butter or apple-sauce is, to me, unthinkable. *One* carefully worked out, pure and classic cheesecake recipe, and one only, is all I'm interested in. To accomplish this, I have studied a hundred recipes and made two hundred cheesecakes—but now that I've done all that, I am content. The result is just one perfect recipe and, for me, it is cheesecake heaven. That is the one I have presented here.

I have the same passion for the classic and simple pound cake. I have developed just one fail-proof recipe for a perfectly wonderful pound cake with a rich aroma and buttery taste. I'm satisfied to make this one recipe forever. The same holds true for the apple pie, the blueberry muffins, the sour-cream coffeecake and the rest of the baking classics presented in this book.

Using only a single, carefully perfected, easy-to-do recipe for each of America's greatest baking classics, I have made it possible for anyone to establish a reputation as a fabulous baker. Welcome to my bakery!

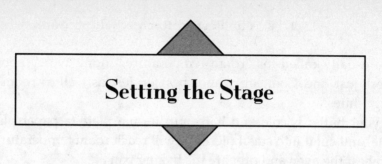

Setting the Stage

Here are a few suggestions that will make your baking a joy instead of a harried and messy nightmare. Before starting to make a recipe:

+ Lay out all of the ingredients your recipe calls for on the counter. It will be reassuring to know that you have everything that you will need.
+ Premeasure the ingredients in the quantities called for, putting the premeasured ingredients into separate dishes, bowls or paper plates. The baking powder, baking soda and salt, when called for, can be added to the flour and mixed together. Then put away the bulk bags, boxes or containers they were stored in. Keep to one side, in their original bottles or containers, the smaller ingredients like vanilla and other extracts, cream of tartar, spices, etc., together with the measuring spoons you will need.
+ If eggs will be added to the batter, break them into a cup first. You don't want to end up with pieces of shell in your batter. If they have to be separated, separate them while they are still cold; it's easier. Also, break the eggs early in the process so they lose a little of their chill before you add them to the batter. If they are still a little cool when you use them, instead of being at

the usually called-for "room temperature," don't worry about it. They'll work just fine. Cool egg whites beat up just as well as room-temperature egg whites.

✦ If your butter is cold and hard, put it on a plate (a paper plate would be fine) and cut it into small pieces. It will reach room temperature quickly.

✦ Preheat the oven and prepare the baking pan.

You are now ready to start mixing the batter with complete concentration on what you are doing. No struggling to get out the proper amount of raisins from a stubborn box or suddenly having to chop up the walnuts while the batter is mixing—or overmixing.

One last helpful hint: When you have a small window of opportunity, clean up as you go along. It will avoid the aggravation of looking at a hopelessly messed-up kitchen after you put the cake in the oven. Baking is much more enjoyable for me when I clean up as I go along. But that's me. Suit yourself and happy baking.

A Few Words About Baking Equipment

To be a good baker you need good baking equipment. Period. This doesn't mean that you have to replace everything you own that doesn't meet the highest professional standards. But as you do make replacement purchases, or add to your collection, take the necessary time to survey what is available to make the best choices.

If possible, buy heavy aluminum or heavy tin-plated steel pans that look good and feel well made. They should have a dull (heat-absorbing) finish instead of a shiny (reflective) finish. Nonstick linings are acceptable as long as the pan is of good solid construction. Glass pans are good and conduct heat so well that the baking time can be reduced a bit. Black-steel, iron and stainless-steel pans are not recommended for reasons of heat conductivity—too much in the case of the first two, and too little in the case of the third. Baking pans with loose, push-up bottoms are great for quickly and easily unmolding cakes after they have cooled. Look for these particularly when purchasing round cake pans and tube pans.

ELECTRIC MIXER

Your most important baking tool will, of course, be a free-standing, heavy-duty, good-quality electric mixer with accompanying bowls, beaters and whisk. It is indispensable for consistently successful results. If you are buying a new one, buy the best one you can afford. Although there are many recipes that can be successfully mixed without the use of an electric mixer, the great majority of them require a mixer if you want to actually enjoy the baking experience. If you don't have a standing mixer, a heavy-duty hand-held one will work just fine.

OVEN THERMOMETER

Make sure you have a good oven thermometer to check the accuracy of your oven settings. It would be such a waste to spend all that time mixing and baking and then have your hopes dashed because your marvelous cake was baking at a temperature that was different from what it was supposed to be. If your oven is off by a small amount, say 10 degrees or 20 degrees, then you can adjust that yourself by setting your oven dial to compensate for the difference. If it is off by a considerably higher amount, then it will pay to have your oven officially calibrated.

MEASURING CUPS AND SPOONS

For dry ingredients you will need a set of measuring cups where the capacity is up to the brim. You can overfill one with a dry ingredient like flour and use a flat knife to level off the top. These are usually made of stainless steel and graduate in size from 1/4 cup to 2 cups. They are worth their weight in gold.

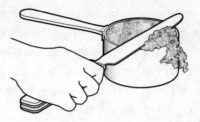

For wet ingredients you will need the usual 1- and 2-cup glass Pyrex cups with measurements marked on the side. Be sure to read them at eye level. If you are looking down on the measuring cup, you will not get an accurate reading.

You will need a set of measuring spoons, also preferably made of stainless steel. I have two sets, which I keep in an attractive mug. It is so reassuring to place this mug on the counter with the measuring ends of all the spoons sticking up in the air waiting to be used. I have two sets so I don't have to wash any out when measuring the wet and then the dry ingredients. I prefer the spoons to be individual spoons and not a group of spoons held together with a metal loop. I find the ones with a metal loop clumsy to use and a nuisance to clean.

PARCHMENT PAPER

Another important thing to have available is a box of baking parchment paper. It's sort of like having a washing machine or a refrigerator. Sure, you can live without it, but it's difficult. For one thing, it makes cookie, scone and biscuit making a breeze. Just place a sheet of parchment paper on your cookie sheet, deposit the cookie, scone or biscuit dough on the paper and bake. It releases instantly from the parchment paper and you don't have to clean the cookie sheet for many bakings to come. Also, to avoid the occasional horror of having your cakes stick to the bottom of the pan, try this trick. Cut out 8- or 9-inch circles of parchment paper (or the proper size oblongs or squares) and fit them into the bottom of the pan. For some recipes you will be greasing and flouring both the bottom and sides of the pan and for other recipes you will be greasing and flouring just the bottom. In either case, this added covering of the bottom with parchment paper is good insurance. Fill the pan with batter, bake and *voilà*! Your cake bottom will never stick. After the cake has cooled, just gently peel the parchment paper from the bottom of the cake. Parchment baking paper is available in many supermarkets and most specialty cookware stores. If you can't find parchment paper, wax paper will do as a substitute.

FLOUR AND SUGAR CANISTERS

It will prove to be very useful to keep your flour in a separate canister and not in the original bag it came in. I keep mine in a large canister and it holds five pounds of flour easily. I also keep my sugar in a smaller canister and it is a great convenience. Small things to do, but they do make your baking life

easier, since these are the two major dry ingredients you'll be constantly using.

SCALE

Not essential but a wonderful convenience. Every professional baker uses a scale. In my recipes I calculate 1 cup of all-purpose flour to weigh 4½ ounces and 1 cup of granulated sugar to weigh 7 ounces. Even if you use a scale to weigh only these two major ingredients, it provides 100 percent accuracy and saves you time.

The following is a list of the weights of some of the more commonly used ingredients called for in this book.

Ingredient	Weight Per Cup
All-purpose flour (spooned and leveled)	4½ ounces
Granulated sugar	7 ounces
Dark brown sugar (firmly packed)	8 ounces
Confectioners' sugar	4½ ounces
Cocoa	3¼ ounces
Walnuts, in small pieces	4 ounces
Dates, chopped	5 ounces
Raisins	5 ounces
Currants	5 ounces
Chocolate chips	6 ounces

The kind of scale I use is a 32-ounce portion-control scale with a turning knob in the center of the round glass face. You can place a plastic bowl of any size, or a paper plate or cup, on the flat top platform, quickly twist the knob so the arrow rests on zero, and then weigh your ingredient immediately, accurately and

easily. This type of portion-control scale is available at restaurant-supply stores.

Other types of scales are also, of course, very useful and easier to obtain. If you do get a scale, make sure it has a weighing capacity of at least 16 ounces, measures by increments of ¼ ounce, and that the container on top has the capacity for two or three cups of flour.

SMALL TOOLS

You will need rubber spatulas; a hand-held pastry blender; one or two pastry brushes; a good, solid, wooden rolling pin; wire whisks; a flour sifter or a sieve with a fairly fine mesh; cake testers and/or a box of round toothpicks or long, thin wooden skewers; a lemon zester or citrus peeler; small plastic bowls; and a stack of paper plates for setting aside premeasured ingredients.

BAKING PANS

A list of baking pans for the serious baker would include:

- ✦ Two round 8-inch-diameter by 1½-inch-deep layer-cake pans.
- ✦ Two round 9-inch-diameter by 1½-inch-deep layer-cake pans.
- ✦ One two-piece round tube pan, either 9-inch diameter (6-cup capacity) or

10-inch diameter (12-cup capacity), with a push-up bottom and either legs or a center tube higher than the sides.

✦ One Bundt pan, either 9-inch diameter or 10-inch diameter, or one of each.
✦ One muffin pan, 12-cup standard size.
✦ One 8 × 8 × 2-inch baking pan.
✦ One springform pan, 8-inch or 9-inch diameter.
✦ Two loaf pans, 9 × 5 × 3 inches or 9 × 4¾ × 2¾ inches or close to it, and two slightly smaller, about 8½ × 4½ × 2½ inches.
✦ One 13 × 9 × 2-inch baking pan.
✦ Two heavy-duty cookie sheets, as large as will fit comfortably in your oven, with at least 1 inch of space all around it.
✦ Two wire cooling racks.
✦ Two 9-inch pie pans, metal (but not stainless steel) or glass, or one of each.

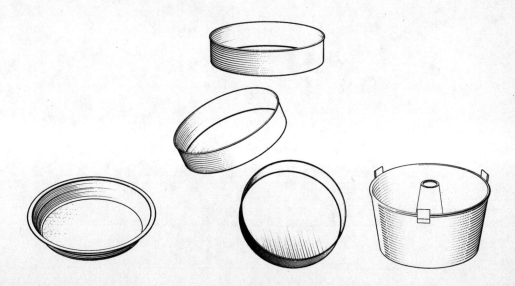

If possible, don't bake a pie in a stainless-steel pie pan. The dough tends not to bake through.

Although this is a fairly complete list, it is certainly not necessary to have everything before you can start turning out delicious, professional-looking baked goods. Use what you have and purchase what you need as you expand your repertoire.

A Few Words About Baking Ingredients

FLOUR

All recipes in this book call for all-purpose flour instead of cake flour. All-purpose flour is milled from a combination of hard and soft wheats and makes excellent baked goods of all types. Cake flour is made from soft wheat, has a lower protein level than all-purpose flour and is often specified in baking recipes, particularly in recipes for chiffon, sponge and angel food–type cakes. I have made many cakes many times with both types of flour and prefer the taste and texture of the ones made with the all-purpose flour.

All-purpose flour is sold both "bleached" and "unbleached" and I recommend using the unbleached flour. The chemical bleaching serves no real purpose other than cosmetic and so I prefer using the more natural version. If your local market sells only bleached all-purpose flour, by all means go ahead and use it. It will make no difference in your baking.

Do not use self-rising flours. They already contain leavening and salt, which calls for too many adjustments in the recipes.

Due to advanced modern milling methods, it is not necessary to sift the

flour unless the recipe specifically requires you to do so. Stirring the dry ingredients together thoroughly is all that is necessary. If the recipe calls for sifting, sift *after* measuring.

To measure cups of flour, I place a measuring cup (one where the 1-cup quantity is up to the very brim) on a paper plate and I spoon the flour from the flour canister into the cup until it overflows the top rim. Then I level it off with the back of a knife or ruler or a flat whatever. This gives me a weight of $4\frac{1}{2}$ ounces per cup. I very often use my scale to reach the required amount of flour. If I need 3 cups of flour, I just weigh up $13\frac{1}{2}$ ounces of flour on my scale ($3 \times 4\frac{1}{2}$ ounces). It's fast and easy and accurate and if you happen to own a scale, I recommend it heartily.

EGGS

All eggs called for in the recipes in this book are large-size eggs, either white or brown.

Large eggs weigh about 2 ounces each in the shell. If all you happen to have at the moment of baking are small, medium, extra-large or jumbo eggs, then you can use the following table to figure out the correct number of eggs to use.

1 small egg weighs	$1\frac{1}{2}$ ounces
1 medium egg weighs	$1\frac{3}{4}$ ounces

1 large egg weighs	2 ounces
1 extra-large egg weighs	2¼ ounces
1 jumbo egg weighs	2½ ounces

You can even use a scale to measure the correct number of different-sized eggs you will need to match the number of 2-ounce (large) eggs called for in the recipe. A very little bit more or less won't make any appreciable difference.

The minute you definitely decide to make a cake, take the correct number of eggs out of the refrigerator and put them on the counter (just as you should do with the butter) so they can start warming up a bit to reach the usually called-for "room temperature" of about 70 degrees. If the recipe calls for separating the eggs, do that while the eggs are still cold, as it's much easier to do then. If you take the eggs right out of the refrigerator and the recipe calls for whole eggs and you really want to get started as soon as possible, you can place them whole in a bowl of warm (not hot) water for about 5 or 10 minutes to hasten the warming-up process. Always keep in mind, however, that cold eggs are easier to separate than warmed-up ones, so, if the eggs are to be separated instead of being used whole, don't go through that warming-up process. Separate the yolks and whites immediately and then let them warm up in their respective bowls.

Many recipes make it almost mandatory to use eggs when they are at room temperature. Eggs taken right out of the refrigerator are at a temperature of about 45 degrees. From my actual experience, egg whites beat up to the same volume when they are fairly cool (55 to 60 degrees), as opposed to their being at about 70 degrees. Whole eggs can also be added to the batter at this in-between, cool temperature; having eggs reach the exact room temperature of 70 degrees is not always absolutely essential.

BUTTER

Nothing can compare to the delicious taste of baked goods made with 100 percent butter. Butter contributes richness, tenderness and flavor to baked goods and, when creamed with sugar, it provides aeration to the finished batter.

All recipes in this book have been formulated with the use of salted butter and not the unsalted butter so enthusiastically recommended in many cookbooks. Unsalted butter is wonderful at the table, on toast, muffins, pancakes, etc., but in a blind tasting of baked goods made with both types of butter, you will not be able to distinguish the difference. For this reason, and because it is easily available, less expensive and doesn't make any difference, salted butter is my choice in baking. If, in spite of this, you have a strong individual preference for unsalted butter, just add a little salt in addition to the salt called for in the recipe. Adding about 1/4 teaspoon of salt for each 4-ounce stick of unsalted butter would be about right.

Do not use whipped butter, margarine or solid vegetable shortening as a substitute for butter. They just won't do the same job. Use only butter sold in sticks or cubes.

In baking, butter is usually used at room temperature (70 degrees), at which point it leaves a slight impression when pressed with a finger. You don't want it too warm, soft or oily as it won't cream properly with the sugar. So don't warm it up in the oven or microwave. If it is too hard and cold when taken from the refrigerator, just unwrap it, put it on a plate (I usually use a paper plate for this purpose) and cut it up into smallish pieces, such as eight slices to a 1/4-pound stick. By the time you get all your other ingredients out and premeasured, the butter will be ready to use.

SUGAR

Sugar provides sweetness, of course, but it also provides aeration to the finished batter when it is creamed with butter. It helps to color the crust during baking and to maintain freshness in the finished cake. Don't add more sugar than the recipe calls for. Too much sugar makes a cake sickeningly sweet instead of delicious and it also interferes with the volume of the cake.

All the recipes in this book calling for granulated sugar refer to the regular, granulated white sugar sold in all markets. Do not use superfine sugar, confectioners' sugar or brown sugar as a substitute for the granulated sugar called for in the recipe. If a different type of sugar is necessary, the recipe will state this.

Unless the granulated sugar is obviously lumpy, it need not be strained. Confectioners' sugar has more of a tendency to lump, so sift it if necessary. Granulated sugar weighs exactly 7 ounces to the cup and, if you own a scale, that's the easiest way to premeasure the amount of sugar you'll need.

BAKING POWDER

All the recipes in this book calling for the use of baking powder require the use of double-acting baking powder, so make sure this is stated on the label. If you are unsure of the freshness of the baking powder you have in the pantry, just put 1 teaspoonful of the powder into about 1/2 cup of hot water and see if it bubbles up fairly vigorously. If it does, it's alive and well, and fine to use.

COCOA

Unsweetened cocoa should be used in baking and not the sweetened and flavored cocoa mixes that take up so much space in the cocoa sections of the

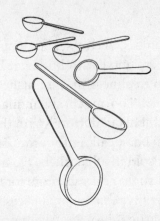

markets. The brands of unsweetened cocoa available nationally are usually Nestlé's, Baker's or Hershey's. These are natural cocoas. The ingredient statement on the container will just say "cocoa."

Another type of cocoa available is called Dutch-process cocoa. This cocoa is treated with a mild alkali to reduce the natural acidity of the cocoa and to darken its color. Brand names for this type of imported cocoa are, among others, Droste and Van Houten. Also, Hershey's has recently introduced a domestic version of this type of cocoa which they designate as "European Style."

If both were easily available to me, I would opt for the Dutch-process cocoa but I would not go to excessive lengths to track it down. You can use either type of cocoa in your baking and get excellent results. Always sift the cocoa powder after measuring it because it has a tendency to lump.

VANILLA EXTRACT, LEMON EXTRACT, GRATED LEMON PEEL, GRATED ORANGE PEEL AND CHOPPED WALNUTS

I recommend that you always use pure vanilla extract and pure lemon extract (or other such pure natural extracts), as opposed to their imitation versions. They add so much to the finished product that it doesn't really pay to take chances with inferior, artificial flavorings.

When grated lemon peel or grated orange peel is called for in a recipe, it means only the colored portion of the lemon or orange and not the white pith that lies underneath. The white pith is quite bitter and you'll wish you hadn't used any. Although you can use a grater for grating up the requisite amount of peel, this is a slow and somewhat messy method of doing it. I use a special small hand tool called a lemon zester or citrus peeler which is inexpensive and is available in cookware stores or cookware departments of department stores. It has one rather large, sharp slot in the center of the tool for peeling off long strips of citrus peel and five tiny sharp circles at the very end of the tool for cutting off tiny strips of peel which can then be minced easily with a sharp knife on a cutting board.

Walnuts are usually found in packages of halves or large pieces and many recipes call for small pieces. The easiest way to solve this problem, for me, is to put the required amount of walnuts in a plastic bag (or a double bag if the plastic seems thin), lay the bag on the counter and then push down on it with my palm, with as much pressure as is needed to break up the large pieces into smaller ones. You can also use the bottom of a small pan or a rolling pin to accomplish the same purpose. Or you can spread the nuts out on a cutting board and chop them with a large, sharp knife.

CAKES

✦ New York Cheesecake ✦

A New York cheesecake is an incredibly elegant, rich and satisfying dessert—providing it is not made into a mishmash with confusing flavors or (I still find it hard to believe this) chocolate chips. The only way to eat it is in small scrapings of the pure, simple and unadorned cake over a long period of time while finishing a cup or two of fresh, strong coffee. Just ask any of the thousands of New Yorkers who did just this at the old and famous Lindy's Restaurant on Broadway in Manhattan. It's the only way to go!

INGREDIENTS

All ingredients must be at room temperature.

For the Graham Cracker Crust (All Sizes)

- 1/4 cup (1/2 stick) salted butter
- 1 1/4 cups graham cracker crumbs
- 1/2 teaspoon cinnamon
- 1 tablespoon granulated sugar

For the Batter

	For a 7-inch pan (serves 8 to 10)	For an 8-inch pan (serves 10 to 12)	For a 9-inch pan (serves 12 to 14)
Cream cheese	16 ounces	24 ounces	32 ounces
Granulated sugar	1/2 cup plus 2 tablespoons	3/4 cup plus 1 tablespoon	1 1/4 cups
Eggs	2	3	4
Egg yolks	2	3	4
Sour cream	1/2 cup	3/4 cup	1 cup
Vanilla	1 tablespoon	1 1/2 tablespoons	2 tablespoons
Lemon juice	1 tablespoon	1 1/2 tablespoons	2 tablespoons

Premeasure and lay out all your ingredients on the counter.

PREPARE YOUR BAKING PAN

Choose a size of springform pan and butter the bottom and sides of it well. Do *not* put a liner on the bottom of the pan as this cake does not turn out after baking and cooling. Since it will be baked in a water bath, ready a large, deep oblong pan (such as a roasting pan) that the springform pan will fit into comfortably, allowing water to surround the pan to the level of at least 1 1/2 inches.

PREHEAT THE OVEN

Set the oven to 350 degrees. Position the rack in the center of the oven.

PREPARING THE CRUST

1. Melt the butter in a small saucepan over low heat.
2. Mix together the graham cracker crumbs, cinnamon and sugar and add

the mixture to the saucepan with the melted butter; toss with a fork or whisk until everything is well blended.

3. Press the prepared crumbs into the bottom of the pan and up the sides (just about an inch or so for the 8-inch and 9-inch pans and a little less for the 7-inch pan) and press firmly. You want some of the cheese filling to show above the crust after it is baked. The given amount of crumbs is just right for the 9-inch pan and you will need a little less for the smaller ones. Place the pan in the refrigerator or freezer while you prepare the batter. The cold crust is less likely to have crumbs that float to the top of the batter as you pour it in.

MIXING THE BATTER

1. In a large bowl, using a mixer, beat the cream cheese with a mixer until it is smooth, soft and creamy.
2. Add the sugar and beat until it is completely incorporated.
3. Add the eggs and egg yolks in two parts, beating until smooth after each addition.
4. Add the sour cream, vanilla and lemon juice and beat until the mixture is smooth and creamy. Scrape down the sides of the bowl several times to

insure a smooth batter. If the batter is still not smooth and creamy, pour it through a strainer. Do not overbeat.

5. Take the springform pan out of the freezer, gently and slowly pour the batter into it, and place in the center of the roasting pan.

6. Pour hot water into the roasting pan so that the water surrounds the springform pan to a depth of about 1½ inches, and put the pan into the oven.

BAKING THE CAKE

Depending on the size of the cheesecake, the baking time will be between 60 and 90 minutes. The best way to tell whether the cake is done is the "shake and shimmy" test. If you move the cake pan just a little bit and the cheese-cake batter shakes and shimmies *just a very little bit* but is not liquidy across the center of the top—that's about right. That's a better test than the clock. The top of the cheesecake, especially around the outer edge, should be turning a medium brown about the time it is fully baked. A completely color-less top isn't quite as appetizing as a top surface that is brown around the edge with the color lightening as it approaches the center. If it isn't browning sufficiently, turn up the oven to 400 degrees and give it a few more minutes, but be careful it doesn't burn. Don't worry about the extra few minutes in the oven; the cheesecake filling will still be creamy and delicious and the top will look professional.

COOLING THE CAKE

Carefully remove the roasting pan from the oven and set it down; remove the springform pan and place it on a cooling rack. After it has cooled for about thirty minutes, release the spring and place the cheesecake, with the bottom of the pan still on, on a serving plate.

SERVING THE CAKE

Refrigerate the cake until ready to serve. Covered with plastic, it will keep beautifully in the refrigerator for three or four days. When slicing the cake (best done before bringing it to the table), use a hot, wet knife. Simply rinse the knife under very hot water *before each slice*.

NOTES

Do not overmix the batter. The reason for using soft cream cheese to start with is to prevent unnecessary beating to get it smooth and creamy. Excess air in the batter has a tendency to make the cake rise and then fall after removal from the oven—resulting in a cracked top surface. The cracks will not affect the taste, but the cake looks nicer with a smooth top.

If the cake starts to get too brown on top before the "shake and shimmy" test tells you that it is done, cover it with an aluminum foil tent.

The cake also freezes beautifully. Carefully wrapped, you can keep it in the freezer for a month or even two and defrost and serve it when you're ready. It would be best to defrost it overnight in the refrigerator.

✦ Angel Food Cake ✦

Angel food cake has no butter, no oil, no egg yolks and no cholesterol and is a favorite of the dieting public. It can be eaten by itself, adorned with fruit or lowfat or nonfat ice cream, frozen yogurt or sherbet for a very special low-fat dessert. As an added dividend, it has an unusually moist and light-as-air texture and is a very delicious treat even for those who are not at all interested in its dietary advantages.

INGREDIENTS

1	cup all-purpose flour
1½	cups granulated sugar
12	large egg whites
1	teaspoon cream of tartar
¼	teaspoon salt
2	teaspoons vanilla
½	teaspoon almond extract (optional)

Premeasure and lay out all your ingredients on the counter.

PREPARE YOUR BAKING PAN

Use an *ungreased* 10-inch tube pan with a removable bottom.

PREHEAT THE OVEN

Set the oven at 350 degrees. Position the rack in the center of the oven.

MIXING THE BATTER

1. In a bowl, sift the flour and half the sugar, gently stir them together and put them aside for later use. Place the remaining sugar next to the mixer for use when you whip up the egg whites.

2. Make sure the egg whites have no pieces of yolk in them and that the bowl and beaters are scrupulously clean. In a large bowl, using a mixer, beat the egg whites for a short time until they are broken up and frothy, and then add the cream of tartar and salt and continue beating at medium speed until the whites form very soft peaks with the tops of the peaks bending over as you lift up the beaters.

3. Continue beating at the same medium speed, while adding a couple of tablespoons of the remaining sugar at a time, beating the mixture for a half minute or so between each addition. After all the sugar is added, continue beating until the mixture forms moist, billowy peaks when you stop the machine and lift out the beaters. The tips of the peaks will either stand up straight or bend over just slightly. Either way is all right. The main thing is to have moist peaks and not overbeaten dry ones.

4. Add the vanilla and beat for a few seconds, until it is incorporated.

5. Remove the bowl and, using a sifter above the bowl, sift in about one third of the flour-sugar mixture and gently fold it in, using a large rubber

spatula, a large whisk or your hand. Repeat this procedure twice more with the remaining flour-sugar mixture.

6. Pour the batter into the *ungreased* pan, smooth out the top, run a sharp knife circularly through the batter a couple of times to remove any air bubbles, smooth the top again and *gently* tap the pan or *gently* drop it on the counter a couple of times.

BAKING THE CAKE

Bake the cake for 40 to 45 minutes until the top is browned, a cake tester or toothpick comes out clean and the top feels springy to the touch. *Do not overbake*. Check often toward the end of the baking time and remove immediately when it is done.

COOLING THE CAKE

If the pan has a higher center or if it has feet, invert it *immediately* upon removal from the oven. If the pan has neither of the above but is completely level on top, invert it on the neck of a sturdy bottle or large funnel. Allow the cake to cool completely for a couple of hours before turning it right side up. Gently remove the cake from the pan by loosening the cake from the sides and the central core with a thin, sharp knife. Do the same with the bottom.

SERVING THE CAKE

When serving the cake, use a serrated knife to cut it.

✦ Chiffon Cake ✦

This very popular cake has a secure place in every baker's repertoire. It is a light and airy cake leavened with beaten eggs and baking powder, and it is also a tender and moist cake because of the addition of vegetable oil. It can be served plain, dusted with confectioners' sugar, or with a scoop of ice cream or a large spoonful of crushed fruit. However you serve it, it will make a hit.

INGREDIENTS

2¼ cups all-purpose flour, measured, then sifted
3 teaspoons baking powder
½ teaspoon salt
1½ cups granulated sugar
½ cup vegetable oil (canola or safflower)
7 large egg yolks
¾ cup orange juice
2 teaspoons grated orange peel
1 teaspoon vanilla
7 large egg whites
½ teaspoon cream of tartar

Premeasure and lay out all your ingredients on the counter.

PREPARE YOUR BAKING PAN

Use a 10-inch round tube pan with a removable bottom and with legs or a high center tube or two 9-inch layer cake pans. *Do not grease the sides of the pans.* If possible, fit a parchment paper liner or wax paper on the bottom of the pan for easier removal of the cooled cake. If you don't use a paper liner,

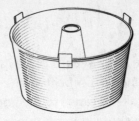

grease with solid shortening and then flour the bottom of the pan only—*not the sides.*

Preheat the Oven

Set the oven to 325 degrees. Position the rack in the center of the oven.

Mixing the Batter

1. In a bowl, sift the flour, baking powder, salt and 1 cup of the sugar, and gently stir them all together.
2. Make a well in the center of the dry ingredients and pour in the vegetable oil, egg yolks, orange juice, orange peel and vanilla. Using a mixer, mix at low speed until all the ingredients are blended together and smooth looking.
3. In another bowl, beat the egg whites until they are frothy. Add the cream of tartar, and then continue mixing until soft, wet peaks are formed, adding the remaining 1/2 cup of sugar gradually as you are mixing. Beat until the peaks stand up straight or bend over just slightly when you lift up the beaters. Do not overbeat. Very stiff, dry egg whites will be difficult to incorporate into the batter.
4. Using a large rubber spatula, fold the egg whites one third at a time

into the batter. Work gently so as to lose as little air as possible from the mixture.

5. When everything has been well blended, push the batter into the baking pan with the spatula, and smooth the top surface evenly. You can gently drop the pan on the counter once or twice, if necessary.

Baking the Cake

Bake the cake for 55 to 65 minutes, until the top is browned and a cake tester or toothpick pushed into the center of the cake comes out clean and the top feels springy to the touch. Do not overbake. Check often toward the end of the baking time and remove immediately when it is done.

Cooling the Cake

If the pan has a higher center or if it has feet, invert it immediately upon removal from the oven. If the pan has neither of the above but is completely level on top, invert it on the neck of a sturdy bottle or funnel. Allow the cake to cool completely before turning it right side up. Gently remove the cake from the pan by loosening from central core and bottom with a thin, sharp knife.

Serving the Cake

When serving the cake, use a serrated knife to cut it.

✦ Sponge Cake ✦

Light, airy, tender, delicate, moist, fragrant are only some of the adjectives commonly used to describe this American classic. It is made without butter or shortening, which is of great appeal to people dedicated to watching their diets, and it is absolutely delicious as well, which is of great appeal to everyone. It can be served alone as a simple but special dessert, or it can be embellished with crushed fruits or berries and/or a dollop of ice cream.

Ingredients

  1   cup all-purpose flour
 1/2 teaspoon salt
  6   large egg yolks
  1   cup granulated sugar
 1/4 cup orange juice
  1   to 2 teaspoons grated orange peel
  1   teaspoon vanilla
  6   large egg whites
 1/2 teaspoon cream of tartar

Premeasure and lay out all your ingredients on the counter.

Prepare Your Baking Pan

Use a 10-inch round tube pan with a removable bottom and with legs or a high center tube or two 9-inch layer cake pans. *Do not grease the sides of the pans.* If possible, fit a parchment paper liner, or wax paper, on the bottom of the pan for easier removal of the cooled cake. If you don't use a paper liner, grease with solid shortening and then flour the bottom of the pan only—*not the sides*.

PREHEAT THE OVEN

Set the oven to 350 degrees. Position the rack in the center of the oven.

MIXING THE BATTER

1. In a bowl, sift the flour and salt together and set aside.
2. Using a mixer, beat the egg yolks at high speed for 6 or 7 minutes until they are thick and lemon-colored. Add ½ cup of the sugar, a few spoonfuls at a time, beating briefly after each addition, about a total of 4 or 5 minutes of mixing. The mixture should be thick, not liquidy. If necessary, continue beating until this happens.
3. Add the orange juice, orange peel and vanilla and blend them in for a few seconds, just until they are incorporated.
4. In a clean bowl, using a mixer, beat the egg whites until they are frothy. Add the cream of tartar and then continue beating until soft, wet (not stiff) peaks are formed. Add the other ½ cup of the sugar and beat until the peaks stand up straight but are still moist looking. Do not overbeat. Very stiff, dry egg whites will be difficult to incorporate into the batter.
5. Using a large rubber spatula, fold the egg whites, one third at a time, into the yolk mixture until both mixtures are blended together.
6. Sprinkle the flour and salt (preferably through a strainer) in three parts over the top of the mixture and fold in each installment gently but thoroughly. Be patient and make sure that small clumps of the flour do not remain unmixed. When pouring the batter into the baking pan, if you notice a small amount of flour still unmixed, use the tip of your spatula to incorporate it.

7. Pour the batter (with the help of the spatula) into the baking pan or pans and even off the top of the batter with the spatula. Drop the pan *gently* on the counter a couple of times to settle the batter evenly.

Baking the Cake

Bake the cake in the tube pan for 30 to 35 minutes, until the top is browned and a cake tester or toothpick inserted in the center comes out clean, without any batter on it. The two round layer cakes should take about 20 minutes. Do not overbake. Check often toward the end of the baking time and remove immediately when it is done.

Cooling the Cake

If the tube pan has a higher center, or if it has feet, invert it on the counter immediately upon removal from the oven. If the tube pan has neither of the above but is completely level on top, invert it on the neck of a sturdy bottle or large funnel. Allow the cake to cool completely before turning the pan right side up. Gently remove the cake from the pan by loosening from the sides with a thin, sharp knife. Allow the cakes in the round pans to cool for about 20 minutes, then turn them out onto a wire rack, right side up, to finish cooling.

Serving the Cake

When serving the cake, use a serrated knife to cut it.

✦ Pound Cake ✦

Pound cake is not only an American classic but an international classic as well. Traditional English recipes called for one pound each of butter, sugar, flour and eggs and this was also the recipe in France, where it was (and still is) known as "Quatre-Quarts," calling for equal parts of the same basic four ingredients. Beating in a sufficient amount of air through the lengthy creaming of the butter and sugar was the key to producing perfect pound cake in earlier times, as it still is today. The air enables the cake to rise. In this recipe, the addition of a small amount of baking powder ensures success. The delicious, buttery taste and the intoxicating aroma of a freshly baked pound cake makes it an inescapable choice for a classic baking repertoire.

INGREDIENTS

2 cups plus 2 tablespoons all-purpose flour
1 teaspoon baking powder
1/2 teaspoon cream of tartar
1/4 teaspoon salt
1/2 teaspoon mace or nutmeg (optional)
1/2 cup milk
2 teaspoons vanilla
8 ounces (2 sticks) salted butter, at room temperature
1 1/4 cups granulated sugar
5 large eggs

Premeasure and lay out all your ingredients on the counter. Lightly combine the flour, baking powder, cream of tartar, salt, and mace or nutmeg. Combine the milk and vanilla.

PREPARE YOUR BAKING PAN

You can use a 9 × 5 × 2½- or 3-inch loaf pan or a 9-inch tube or Bundt pan. Spray the inside of the pan with nonstick spray (PAM or something similar) or grease the pan with solid shortening and dust with flour, tapping out the excess flour. It would also be helpful (but not essential) to cut out a piece of parchment or wax paper the size of the pan bottom and lay it in. It makes removing the cake from the pan a bit easier.

PREHEAT THE OVEN

Set the oven to 350 degrees. Position the rack in the center of the oven.

MIXING THE BATTER

1. In a large bowl, using a mixer, beat the butter at high speed until it is soft and smooth, about 1 minute.
2. Add the sugar in two parts and continue beating, at medium speed, after each addition until the mixture is light and fluffy. Total mixing time, including scraping down the bowl with a large rubber spatula once or twice, is about 4 to 5 minutes.

3. At medium speed, add the eggs one at a time, beating only until they are well blended. Remember to scrape down the bowl once or twice. Don't worry if the batter looks curdled; when the flour is added it will become smooth.

4. Add one third of the dry ingredients and one third of the milk-vanilla mixture and mix at medium speed for about 20 seconds. Do this twice more and then beat the batter for about 1 minute or so until it is uniform and smooth looking. Do not overbeat.

5. Spoon the batter into the cake pan, then level the top with a spoon or spatula. Dropping the pan gently once or twice on the counter will also help level it.

BAKING THE CAKE

Bake for 60 or 65 minutes until cake is browned and a cake tester or toothpick pushed into the very center of the cake comes out clean, without any batter on it. Pay particular attention to the very top center of the cake (where the split is), putting your cake tester in sideways and shallowly to make sure the cake is done to the very top. Because this is a dense cake, this is a more reliable test than touching a finger to the top. Just make sure the cake in the center of the split looks dry. If in doubt, bake it a couple of minutes longer. If the top starts to look too brown toward the end of the baking period, cover it with an aluminum foil tent.

COOLING THE CAKE

Allow the cake to cool in the pan for about 20 minutes, then turn it out onto a wire rack, right side up, to finish cooling.

VARIATIONS

Lemon Poppy-Seed Pound Cake

Add 5 tablespoons of poppy seeds, 1 tablespoon of grated lemon peel and 1 tablespoon of lemon extract to the batter. Use just 1 teaspoon of vanilla instead of 2 teaspoons.

Marble Pound Cake

Add 3 tablespoons of unsweetened cocoa blended with 4 tablespoons of sugar to 1 cup of the finished batter and then fill the baking pan with the batters, alternating large spoonfuls of the light-colored batter with small spoonfuls of the chocolate batter. When finished, swirl a knife blade through the batter a few times to create the marbling.

✦ Boston Cream Pie ✦

Not a pie at all, but who cares? It's luscious and wonderful and a real American classic. It originated in Colonial times as a pudding cake. Then the famous Parker House Hotel in Boston had the brilliant idea of putting a dark, shiny chocolate glaze on top and *voilà*, we have a delicious golden cake, split and filled with a creamy vanilla custard and then topped with a chocolate glaze. Cakes just can't get any better than that. Incidentally, if you fill it with raspberry preserves and then dust it with confectioners' sugar, you end up with a Washington Pie. Try it both ways (on different occasions, of course) and see which one you prefer. Be extra sure to read this recipe all the way through, since it's a long one—and worth every minute!

MAKING THE CAKE

Ingredients

- 1½ cups all-purpose flour
- 2¼ teaspoons baking powder
- ¼ teaspoon salt
- ½ cup plus 2 tablespoons milk
- 1 teaspoon vanilla
- 4 ounces (1 stick) salted butter, at room temperature
- 1 cup granulated sugar
- 2 large eggs
- 1 large egg yolk

Premeasure and lay out all your ingredients on the counter. Lightly combine the flour, baking powder and salt. In a separate bowl combine the milk and vanilla.

PREPARE YOUR BAKING PAN

Use a 9-inch round pan. Spray the inside of the pan with nonstick spray (PAM or something similar) or grease the pan with solid shortening and dust with flour, tapping out the excess flour. It would also be helpful (but not essential) to cut out a piece of parchment or wax paper the size of the pan bottom and lay it in. It makes removing the cake from the pan a bit easier.

PREHEAT THE OVEN

Set the oven to 350 degrees. Position the rack in the center of the oven.

MIXING THE BATTER

1. In a large bowl, using a mixer, beat the butter at high speed until it is soft and smooth, about 1 minute.
2. Add the sugar in two parts and continue beating, at medium speed, after each addition until the mixture is light and fluffy. Total mixing time, including scraping down the bowl with a large rubber spatula once or twice, is 4 to 5 minutes.
3. At medium speed, add the eggs and egg yolk in two parts, beating only until they are well blended. Remember to scrape down the bowl once or twice.
4. Add half of the dry ingredients and half of the milk-vanilla mixture and mix at medium speed for about 20 seconds. Do this one more time and then beat the batter for about 1 minute or so, until it is uniform and smooth looking. Do not overbeat.
5. Pour the batter into the cake pan. Then level the top with a spoon or spatula. Dropping the pan gently once or twice on the counter will help level it.

BAKING THE CAKE

Bake the cake 35 to 45 minutes. Check several times toward the end of the baking time. Do not overbake. The top should be browned and springy to the touch and a cake tester or toothpick inserted into the center of the cake should come out clean, without any batter on it.

COOLING THE CAKE

Allow the cake to cool in the pan for about 20 minutes, then turn it out onto a wire rack, right side up, to finish cooling. When completely cool, carefully cut it in half horizontally so that you will have two thin layers.

MAKING THE VANILLA CUSTARD FILLING

Ingredients

- ³/₄ cup milk
- ¹/₂ cup heavy whipping cream
- 6 tablespoons granulated sugar
- 2 tablespoons cornstarch
- ¹/₈ teaspoon salt
- 2 large egg yolks
- 1 teaspoon vanilla

Cooking the Custard

1. Put the milk and cream into a saucepan.
2. In a bowl, stir together thoroughly the sugar, cornstarch and the salt until no lumps of cornstarch remain and then add to the saucepan, mixing everything together.
3. Lightly beat the egg yolks and add to the saucepan.
4. Cook this mixture over medium heat, stirring from time to time while mixture is heating. When it begins to get hot, start stirring continuously.
5. The custard will start to thicken as it gets hotter and reaches a slow boil with bubbles beginning to break in the middle. Let it boil quietly for about 1 minute and then immediately remove it from the heat. If it starts to boil too strongly during the last minute of boiling, just lift the saucepan a little above the heat while continuing to stir. The mixture should be quite thick when you take it off the heat. If it seems to be fairly thick in less than 1 minute, you can remove it from the heat.
6. Add the vanilla and stir.
7. Put a piece of plastic wrap, with a couple of slits in it, directly on top of the custard to prevent a skin from forming.
8. Cool for about 30 minutes before using.

Making the Chocolate Icing

Ingredients

1 ounce (1 square) unsweetened chocolate
2 tablespoons water
2 tablespoons salted butter
1/2 teaspoon vanilla
1 cup confectioners' sugar

PREPARING THE ICING

1. Put chocolate, water and butter in a small saucepan and, stirring, melt them together over low heat. Remove the saucepan from the heat.
2. Add the vanilla.
3. Whisk in the confectioners' sugar. If needed, add 1 teaspoon of hot water at a time until the icing is smooth and of spreading consistency. Use the icing while it is still warm.

ASEMBLING THE CAKE

1. Spread the custard filling evenly on top of one of the layers of cake and then cover that layer with the second layer.
2. Spread the chocolate icing on top of the cake with a spatula, spreading it to the very edge.
3. Refrigerate the cake until ready to serve.

✦ Carrot Cake ✦

This is a thoroughly American invention that has succeeded in captivating the hearts of everyone, everywhere. It is a moist and luscious cake, and its enthusiastic reception will make the job of grating fresh carrots worth the effort. Keep it in mind for that very "special" occasion because this is a very special cake, especially if topped with Cream-Cheese Icing.

INGREDIENTS

- 1¼ cups vegetable oil (canola or safflower)
- 2 cups granulated sugar
- 4 large eggs
- 2 cups all-purpose flour
- 3 teaspoons baking powder
- 1 teaspoon baking soda
- 2 teaspoons cinnamon
- ¼ teaspoon nutmeg
- ¼ teaspoon allspice
- ½ teaspoon salt
- 4 cups (about 1 pound) grated or shredded carrots, firmly packed
- 1 8-ounce can crushed pineapple, packed in unsweetened pineapple juice, drained well
- 1 cup walnuts, in small pieces
- 1 teaspoon vanilla
- 1 cup raisins

Premeasure and lay out all your ingredients on the counter.

PREPARE YOUR BAKING PAN

Use a 13 × 9 × 2-inch baking pan or two 9-inch layer-cake pans. Spray the inside of the pan with nonstick spray (PAM or something similar) or grease the pan with solid shortening and dust with flour, tapping out the excess flour. It would also be helpful (but not essential) to cut out a piece of parchment or wax paper the size of the pan bottom and lay it in. It makes removing the cake from the pan a bit easier.

PREHEAT THE OVEN

Set the oven to 350 degrees. Position the rack in the center of the oven.

MIXING THE BATTER

1. In a large bowl, using a mixer, beat together the vegetable oil and sugar.
2. Add the eggs and beat the mixture at high speed for 2 or 3 minutes to help aerate it.
3. In a separate bowl, mix together the flour, baking powder, baking soda, cinnamon, nutmeg, allspice and salt and add them to the mixing bowl. Beat at low speed for about 1 minute.
4. Add the carrots, crushed pineapple, walnuts, vanilla and raisins and blend them in until the batter is uniform in appearance.
5. Pour the batter into the baking pan and level the top with a spatula or spoon.

BAKING THE CAKE

Bake for 40 to 50 minutes if you are using a 13 × 9 × 2-inch pan, less if you are using layer-cake pans. Bake until the top is browned and feels springy to the touch and a cake tester or toothpick comes out clean, without any batter on it.

COOLING THE CAKE

The 13 × 9 × 2-inch cake can be cooled in, iced in, and served right out of the pan. Allow the cakes in the round pans to cool for about 20 minutes, then turn them out onto a wire rack, right side up, to finish cooling.

MAKING THE CREAM-CHEESE ICING

Ingredients

2 ounces (1/2 stick) salted butter, at room temperature
8 ounces cream cheese, at room temperature
1 teaspoon vanilla
2 cups (about half a 1-pound box) confectioners' sugar

Beat the butter and cream cheese until very soft and very smooth. Add the vanilla and the powdered sugar and beat at high speed until the icing is smooth and creamy.

ICING THE CAKE

Using a spatula or broad knife, spread the icing evenly over the top and along the sides of the 13 × 9 × 2-inch cake; do the same with the round layer cake, this time including icing in between the layers and on the sides. Refrigerate before serving.

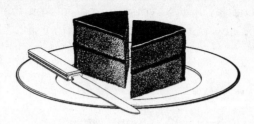

✦ Chocolate Cake ✦

For chocolate fanatics no cake can compare with a real, honest-to-goodness chocolaty chocolate cake and I sometimes find myself leaning in that direction. Served by itself, with or without ice cream, or made into a layer cake filled with chocolate frosting and covered with a dark chocolate glaze, this recipe should satisfy anyone's need for a chocolate fix.

INGREDIENTS

2	cups all-purpose flour
1½	teaspoons baking powder
1	teaspoon baking soda
½	teaspoon salt
1½	cups cold water
1	teaspoon vanilla
½	cup vegetable oil (canola or safflower)
2	cups granulated sugar
2	large eggs
½	cup unsweetened cocoa, measured, then sifted

Premeasure and lay out all your ingredients on the counter. Lightly combine the flour, baking powder, baking soda and salt. Combine the water and vanilla.

Prepare Your Baking Pan

You can use two 8- or 9-inch round pans or a 13 × 9 × 2-inch oblong pan. Spray the inside of the pan with a nonstick spray (PAM or something similar) or grease the pan with solid shortening and dust with flour. Tap out excess flour. It would also be helpful (but not essential) to cut out a piece of parchment or wax paper the size of the pan bottom and lay it in. It makes removing the cake from the pans a bit easier.

Preheat the Oven

Set the oven to 350 degrees. Position the rack in the center of the oven.

Mixing the Batter

1. In a large bowl, using a mixer, beat together the vegetable oil, sugar and eggs until they are smooth and uniform in appearance.
2. Add the sifted cocoa. To prevent getting a big puff of cocoa when you turn on the mixer, before you start the mixer stir with a spatula. Start the mixer, using the lowest possible speed, and then beat at medium speed until the mixture is smooth.
3. Add one third of the dry ingredients and about one third of the water-vanilla mixture. To prevent getting a big puff of flour or splash of water when you turn on the mixer, stir with the spatula before you start it. Start the mixer and beat at medium speed until the mixture is smooth, about

20 seconds. Do this two more times and then beat the batter for about 1 minute or so, until it is uniform and smooth. It will be quite thin.

4. Pour the batter into the round pans or oblong pan.

BAKING THE CAKE

Bake the round cakes for 30 to 35 minutes and the oblong cake a little longer, until the top feels springy to the touch and a cake tester or toothpick inserted into the center of the cake comes out clean, without any batter on it.

SERVING THE CAKE

In order to serve the cake right out of the oblong pan, let the pan cool on a wire rack for about 20 minutes, and pour a warm icing over the warm cake, tilting the pan so that the icing covers it evenly. The Chocolate Fudge Frosting, while still warm and pourable, would be a good choice. (See "Frostings and Glazes.")

TO MAKE A LAYER CAKE

Allow the round cakes to cool in the pan for about 20 minutes, then turn them out onto a wire rack, right side up, to finish cooling. A good frosting to use would be the same Chocolate Fudge Frosting mentioned above, but cooled to spreading consistency.

✦ Devil's Food Cake ✦

This version of a chocolate cake uses unsweetened chocolate instead of the usual cocoa, plus dark brown sugar and buttermilk, to create a rich, moist, delicious chocolate cake that is guaranteed to satisfy any chocolate lover.

INGREDIENTS

2	cups all-purpose flour
1	teaspoon baking powder
1	teaspoon baking soda
1/4	teaspoon salt
3	ounces unsweetened chocolate
4	ounces (1 stick) salted butter, at room temperature
1 1/2	cups dark brown sugar, firmly packed
3	large eggs
2	teaspoons vanilla
1	cup buttermilk
1/4	cup water

Premeasure and lay out all your ingredients on the counter. Lightly combine the flour, baking powder, baking soda and salt.

PREPARE YOUR BAKING PAN

You can use two 9-inch round pans, a 13 × 9 × 2-inch oblong pan, a Bundt pan or a 10-inch tube pan. Spray the inside of the pan with nonstick spray (PAM or something similar) or grease the pan with solid shortening and dust with flour, tapping out the excess flour. It would also be helpful (but not essential) to cut out a piece of parchment or wax paper the size of the pan bottom (except for the Bundt pan) and lay it in. It makes removing the cake from the pan a bit easier.

PREHEAT THE OVEN

Set the oven to 350 degrees. Position the rack in the center of the oven.

MIXING THE BATTER

1. Melt the chocolate by stirring it in the top of a double boiler over simmering, not boiling water. Or stir it in a small bowl that just sits in the top of a small saucepan without touching the simmering water in the saucepan. Or put it in a microwave-safe bowl, cover it with wax paper or plastic wrap, put the bowl in the microwave and turn the microwave on high. After 1 minute, check it every 15 seconds until it's mostly melted. Then stir until melting is complete. In all cases, you don't want the chocolate to get too hot—it will burn. Try to finish the melting by stirring the last few remaining small pieces of chocolate while it is away from the heat. When the chocolate is melted, put it aside.

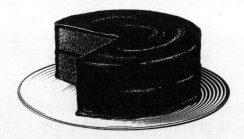

2. In a large bowl, using a mixer, beat the butter at high speed until it is soft and smooth, about 1 minute.
3. Add the sugar in two parts and continue beating, at medium speed, after each addition until the mixture is light and fluffy. Total mixing time, including scraping down the bowl with a large rubber spatula once or twice, is about 4 to 5 minutes.
4. At medium speed, add the eggs one at a time, beating only until they are well blended. Remember to scrape down the bowl once or twice.
5. Mix in the melted chocolate and the vanilla.
6. Add a third of the dry ingredients and a third of the buttermilk and mix at medium speed for about 20 seconds. Do this two more times and then beat for about 1 minute or so, until the batter is uniform and smooth looking. Do not overbeat.
7. Add the water and blend it in.
8. Pour the batter into cake pans or pan, then level the top of the batter. Dropping the pans gently once or twice on the counter will help level it.

BAKING THE CAKE

Bake the cake about 30 minutes for the 9-inch round pans, 40 to 45 minutes for the 13 × 9 × 2-inch oblong pan and 55 to 60 minutes for the 10-inch tube pan. Check several times toward the end of the baking period. Do not overbake. The top should be springy to the touch and a cake tester or toothpick inserted into the center should come out clean, without any batter on it.

COOLING THE CAKE

Allow the cakes to cool in the pans for about 20 minutes, then turn them out onto a wire rack, right side up, to finish cooling.

Serving the Cake

A portion of this cake dusted with confectioners' sugar and served with or without a scoop of vanilla ice cream is obviously a delicious looking and tasting dessert. To gild the lily, however, and make it really sensational, frost it with Very Special Chocolate Fudge Icing. (See "Frostings and Glazes.")

✦ Cupcakes ✦

MAKES APPROXIMATELY 12 CUPCAKES

There's something especially mouthwatering about cupcakes topped with frosting. They can be made in various sizes to suit the occasion and frosted in many ways to satisfy the imagination. Many cake recipes make delicious cupcakes, but this recipe makes absolutely the *most* delicious cupcakes. See "Frostings and Glazes" for topping choices.

INGREDIENTS

$1\frac{1}{4}$ cups all-purpose flour
2   teaspoons baking powder
$\frac{1}{4}$ teaspoon cream of tartar
$\frac{1}{8}$ teaspoon salt
$\frac{1}{2}$ cup plus 2 tablespoons milk
$1\frac{1}{2}$ teaspoons vanilla
3   ounces ($\frac{3}{4}$ stick) salted butter, at room temperature
$\frac{2}{3}$ cup granulated sugar
2   large eggs

Premeasure and lay out all your ingredients on the counter. Lightly combine the flour, baking powder, cream of tartar and salt. Combine the milk and vanilla.

PREPARE YOUR BAKING PAN

Put paper cupcake liners into a twelve-cup standard-size muffin pan. The

paper liners make removal of the baked cupcakes easy, make cleanup easier and help the cupcakes stay fresh longer.

PREHEAT THE OVEN

Set the oven to 400 degrees (to be turned down to 375 degrees after the cupcakes are put in.) Position the rack in the center of the oven. Place a cookie sheet on top of the rack to prevent overbrowning of cupcake bottoms.

MIXING THE BATTER

1. In a large bowl, using a mixer, beat the butter at high speed until it is soft and smooth, about 1 minute.
2. Add the sugar in two parts and continue beating at medium speed after each addition until the mixture is light and fluffy.
3. At medium speed, add the eggs, beating only until they are well blended. Remember to scrape down the bowl once or twice.
4. Add one half of the dry ingredients and one half of the milk and vanilla mixture and mix at medium speed for about 20 seconds. Add the other half in the same way and then beat the batter for about 1 minute or so,

until it is uniform and smooth looking. Scrape down the sides of the mixing bowl once or twice while the batter is mixing. Do not overbeat.

5. Using a large spoon or a large ice-cream scoop, drop the batter into the paper muffin cups until they are three-fourths to seven-eighths full. Do not fill to the top.

BAKING THE CUPCAKES

Turn down the oven to 375 degrees after the cupcakes are put in. Bake for 25 to 30 minutes until the tops of the cupcakes are lightly browned, the cupcakes feel springy to the touch and a cake tester or toothpick comes out clean, without any batter on it.

COOLING THE CUPCAKES

Cool the cupcakes in the pan for about 10 minutes, then lift them out and put them on a wire rack to finish cooling.

FROSTING THE CUPCAKES

Please see "Frostings and Glazes."

✦ Gingerbread ✦

"Gyngebreed" was mentioned in Chaucer's fourteenth-century *Canterbury Tales* and Colonial housewives were baking it during the American Revolution. The best thing about gingerbread is a warm slice of the dark, pungent, rich, molasses-flavored cake waiting for you shortly after it comes out of the oven. For an elegant dessert, serve it with dollops of whipped cream or vanilla ice cream. People go crazy for homemade gingerbread.

INGREDIENTS

1²/₃	cups all-purpose flour
1	teaspoon baking soda
¹/₄	teaspoon salt
2	teaspoons ginger
³/₄	teaspoon cinnamon
¹/₈	teaspoon ground cloves
3	ounces (³/₄ stick) salted butter, at room temperature
¹/₂	cup dark brown sugar (light brown may be substituted)
¹/₂	cup molasses (light is preferred but dark may be used)
1	large egg
²/₃	cup hot water

Premeasure and lay out all your ingredients on the counter. Lightly combine the flour, baking soda, salt, ginger, cinnamon and cloves.

PREPARE YOUR BAKING PAN

You can use an 8 × 8 × 2-inch or a 9 × 9 × 2-inch square baking pan. Spray the inside of the pan with nonstick spray (PAM or something similar) or grease the pan with solid shortening and dust with flour, tapping out the excess flour. It would also be helpful (but not essential) to cut out a piece of parchment or wax paper the size of the pan bottom and lay it in. It makes removing the cake from the pan a bit easier.

Preheat the Oven

Set the oven to 350 degrees. Position the rack in the center of the oven.

Mixing the Batter

1. In a large bowl, using a mixer, beat the butter at high speed until it is soft and smooth, about 1 minute.
2. Add the sugar in two parts. Continue beating, at medium speed, after each addition until the mixture is light and fluffy. Total mixing time, including scraping down the bowl with a large rubber spatula once or twice, is about 4 to 5 minutes.
3. Add the molasses and just blend it in.
4. At medium speed, add the egg, beating only until it is well blended. Remember to scrape down the bowl once or twice.
5. Add half of the dry ingredients and half of the hot water, and mix at medium speed for about 20 seconds. Do this one more time and then beat the batter for about 1 minute or so, until it is uniform and smooth looking. Do not overbeat.
6. Spoon the batter into the cake pan, then level the top with a spoon or spatula. Dropping the pan gently once or twice on the counter will help level it.

Baking the Cake

Bake the cake for 35 to 45 minutes, until the top is browned and feels springy to the touch and a cake tester or toothpick inserted into the center comes out clean, without any batter on it.

Cooling the Cake

Allow the cake to cool in the pan for about 20 minutes, then turn it out onto a wire rack, right side up, to finish cooling. If you prefer, serve squares of the cake right out of the pan.

✦ Golden Yellow Cake ✦

This is a no-fail, basic cake that derives from the original pound cake recipe, with some additional leavening and liquid. It is a tender cake with a delicious taste which makes it a great, easy-to-do foundation cake for all the icings and frostings you can dream up. A wedge of plain cake, dusted with a sprinkling of confectioners' sugar, is also a treat.

INGREDIENTS

3	cups all-purpose flour
4$\frac{1}{2}$	teaspoons baking powder
$\frac{1}{2}$	teaspoon salt
8	ounces (2 sticks) salted butter, at room temperature
2	cups granulated sugar
4	large eggs
2	large egg yolks
1$\frac{1}{4}$	cups milk
2	teaspoons vanilla

Premeasure and lay out all your ingredients on the counter. Lightly combine the flour, baking powder and salt. Combine the milk and vanilla.

Prepare Your Baking Pan

You can use two 9-inch round pans, a 13 × 9 × 2-inch oblong pan or a 10-inch two-piece tube pan. Spray the inside of the pan with nonstick spray (PAM or something similar) or grease the pan with solid shortening and dust with flour, tapping out the excess flour. It would also be helpful (but not essential) to cut out a piece of parchment or wax paper the size of the pan bottom and lay it in. It makes removing the cake from the pan a bit easier.

Preheat the Oven

Set the oven to 350 degrees. Position the rack in the center of the oven.

Mixing the Batter

1. In a large bowl, using a mixer, beat the butter at high speed until it is soft and smooth, about 1 minute.
2. Add the sugar in two parts and continue beating, at medium speed, after each addition until the mixture is light and fluffy. Total mixing time, including scraping down the bowl with a large rubber spatula once or twice, is 4 to 5 minutes.
3. At medium speed, add the eggs and yolks two at a time, beating only until they are well blended. Remember to scrape down the bowl once or twice.
4. Add a third of the dry ingredients and a third of the milk-vanilla mixture and mix at medium speed for about 20 seconds. Do this two more times and then beat the batter for about 1 minute or so, until it is uniform and smooth looking. Do not overbeat.
5. Spoon the batter into the cake pans or pan, then level the top of the batter

with a spoon or spatula. Dropping the pan gently once or twice on the counter will help level it.

BAKING THE CAKE

Bake the cake 30 to 35 minutes for the 9-inch round pans, 35 to 40 minutes for the oblong pan and 55 to 60 minutes for the tube pan. Check several times toward the end of the baking period. Do not overbake. The top should be browned and springy to the touch and a cake tester or toothpick inserted into the center of the cake should come out clean, without any batter on it.

COOLING THE CAKE

Allow the cake to cool in the pan for about 20 minutes, then turn it out onto a wire rack, right side up, to finish cooling.

✦ Strawberry Shortcake ✦

The joys of summer are never complete without at least one strawberry shortcake to feast on slowly and lingeringly. The combination of fragrant red, ripe strawberries decorating mounds of cold, freshly whipped sweet cream on top of a wonderful golden cake makes this the queen of summer treats. Although some may opt for sweetened biscuits as the base of the luscious cake, I think it tastes much better this way.

INGREDIENTS

For the Cake Layers

- 1 cup all-purpose flour, measured, then sifted
- 1/2 teaspoon salt
- 6 large egg yolks
- 1 cup granulated sugar
- 1/4 cup milk
- 1 teaspoon vanilla
- 6 large egg whites
- 1/2 teaspoon cream of tartar

For the Strawberries and Whipped Cream

- 1 pint heavy whipping cream
- 4 cups sweet, red, ripe strawberries
- 1/4 cup confectioners' sugar
- 1/2 teaspoon vanilla

Premeasure and lay out all your ingredients on the counter. Put the heavy cream in a medium-size bowl to chill in the refrigerator.

PREPARE YOUR BAKING PANS

Use two 8-inch or 9-inch layer-cake pans. *Do not grease the sides of the pans.* If possible, fit a parchment paper liner, or wax paper, on the bottom of each pan for easier removal of the cooled cake. If you don't use paper liners, grease with solid shortening and then flour the bottom of the pans only—*not the sides.*

PREHEAT THE OVEN

Set the oven to 350 degrees. Position the rack in the center of the oven.

MIXING THE BATTER

1. In a bowl, sift the flour and salt together and set aside.
2. Using a mixer, beat the egg yolks at high speed for 6 or 7 minutes until they are thick and lemon-colored. Add 1/2 cup of the sugar, a few spoonfuls at a time, beating briefly after each addition, about a total of 4 or 5 minutes of mixing. The mixture should be thick, not liquidy. If necessary, continue beating until this happens.
3. Add the milk and vanilla and blend them in for a few seconds, just until they are incorporated.
4. In a clean bowl, using clean beaters, beat the egg whites until they are frothy. Add the cream of tartar and then continue beating until soft, moist

peaks are formed. Add the other ½ cup of the sugar and beat until the peaks stand up straight but are still moist looking. Do not overbeat. Very stiff, dry egg whites will be difficult to incorporate into the batter.

5. Using a large rubber spatula, fold the egg whites, one third at a time, into the yolk mixture until both mixtures are blended together.

6. Sprinkle the flour and salt (preferably through a strainer) in three parts over the top of the mixture and fold in each third gently but thoroughly. Be patient and make sure that small clumps of the flour do not remain unmixed. When pouring the batter into the baking pans, if you notice a small amount of flour still unmixed, use the tip of your spatula to incorporate it.

7. Pour the batter (with the help of the spatula) into the baking pans and even the top of the batter with the spatula. Drop the pan gently on the counter a couple of times to settle the batter evenly.

BAKING THE CAKE

Bake the cake for 20 to 25 minutes, until the top is browned and a cake tester or toothpick inserted in the center comes out clean, without any batter on it. Do not overbake.

COOLING THE CAKE

Allow the cake to cool in the pan for about 20 minutes, then turn it out onto a wire rack, right side up, to finish cooling.

PREPARING THE STRAWBERRIES

You will have already bought two one-pint boxes of the ripest, reddest and most beautiful strawberries in the marketplace. After you wash and hull them (remove the leaves), lay them out on a paper towel to dry. Cut each strawberry in half. Leave a few whole berries to decorate the top. If, in spite of how they look, they just aren't sweet enough, you can lightly sprinkle some sugar over them. After a few minutes, taste one just to make sure.

PREPARING THE WHIPPED CREAM

Beat the cream in the chilled bowl until it is frothy. Add the confectioners' sugar and vanilla and continue beating until stiff peaks have formed. When you lift up the beaters, the peaks should stand up straight. Then stop immediately: You don't want butter.

ASSEMBLING THE CAKE

Put one of the cake layers on a large serving plate. Cover the top with half of the whipped cream and evenly distribute half of the strawberries on it. Put the second layer on top, press it down gently, put on the remaining whipped cream and smooth it down with a spatula. Decorate the top with any remaining strawberries. Refrigerate until serving time but not more than 2 hours; this cake is best when it's assembled shortly before serving. You will have to decide what to do with any leftover strawberries and whipped cream!

✦ Blueberry Coffee Cake ✦

The obvious choice to use in this cake is fresh, plump, ripe blueberries—one of summer's most delightful gifts. However, you can also use frozen whole berries, providing they are quick-frozen without added sugar or syrup, and thus create this warm memory of summer's bounty at any time of the year. This is simple, easy to make and delicious.

INGREDIENTS

- 3 cups all-purpose flour
- 2 teaspoons baking powder
- 1/2 teaspoon baking soda
- 1/2 teaspoon salt
- 4 ounces (1 stick) salted butter, at room temperature
- 1 1/2 cups granulated sugar
- 3 large eggs
- 2 teaspoons vanilla
- 1 cup sour cream
- 2 to 2 1/2 cups blueberries, fresh or unsweetened frozen (If frozen, do *not* defrost before using. If fresh, rinse and gently dry.)
- Confectioners' sugar for garnish (optional)

Premeasure and lay out all your ingredients on the counter. Lightly combine the flour, baking powder, baking soda and salt.

PREPARE YOUR BAKING PAN

For the most attractive appearance, use a 9-inch Bundt pan, about 4 inches deep (approximately 10-cup capacity). Or you can use a 10-inch Bundt pan

(12-cup capacity) or a 10 × 4-inch round tube pan. Spray the inside of the pan with nonstick spray (PAM or something similar) or generously grease the pan with solid shortening and dust with flour, tapping out the excess flour. Be especially careful to spray or grease the Bundt pan thoroughly, including all the nooks and crannies. If greasing, a small, soft pastry brush can be very helpful. Flour the center tube by tossing a little flour on it from the tip of a teaspoon.

Preheat the Oven

Set the oven to 350 degrees. Position the rack in the center of the oven.

Mixing the Batter

1. In a large bowl, using a mixer, beat the butter at high speed until it is soft and smooth, about 1 minute.
2. Add the sugar in two parts and continue beating, at medium speed, after each addition until the mixture is light and fluffy. Total mixing time, including scraping down the bowl with a large rubber spatula once or twice, is 4 to 5 minutes.

3. At medium speed, add the eggs one at a time, beating only until they are well blended. Remember to scrape down the bowl once or twice.
4. Add a third of the dry ingredients, all the vanilla and a third of the sour cream and mix at medium speed for about 20 seconds. Do this two more times and then beat the batter for about 1 minute or so until it is uniform and smooth looking. Do not overbeat.
5. Gently and carefully dust the blueberries with flour, turning them over with a large spoon, and then with a large spatula, fold them into the batter.
6. With the help of the spatula, pour the batter into the baking pan. The batter should fill the pan at least to the halfway mark but be no more than three-quarters full.

BAKING THE CAKE

Bake the cake 60 to 75 minutes (a lot depends on the type of Bundt pan you use), until the top is nicely browned and feels springy to the touch and a cake tester or toothpick comes out clean, without any batter on it. The latter is a more important test than watching the clock.

COOLING THE CAKE

Allow the cake to cool in the pan for about 20 minutes, then turn it out onto a wire rack, right side up, to finish cooling.

SERVING THE CAKE

Before serving the cake you can simply dust it evenly with confectioners' sugar or you can drizzle a simple glaze over it. (See "Frostings and Glazes.")

✦ Fresh Apple Coffee Cake ✦

As everyone knows, all coffee cakes are wonderful and this one is no exception. It is a moist cake, fragrant with the smell of fresh apples and the added notes of cinnamon and brown sugar. It lasts a long time, too, in or out of the refrigerator—if you let it.

INGREDIENTS

For the Apple Mixture

Use tart cooking apples such as Granny Smith, Gravenstein, Baldwin, Pippin, Northern Spy or, less tart but still good to use, Golden Delicious.

3 to 4 cups apples, cored and cut up into 1/2-inch dice (I prefer unpeeled apples but peeled apples are perfectly fine, too, if that is your preference.)
1/2 cup dark brown sugar, firmly packed
1 teaspoon cinnamon
3/4 cup walnuts, in small pieces

For the Cake

- 3 cups all-purpose flour
- 2 teaspoons baking powder
- 1/2 teaspoon baking soda
- 1/2 teaspoon salt
- 4 ounces (1 stick) salted butter, at room temperature
- 1 1/2 cups granulated sugar
- 3 large eggs
- 2 teaspoons vanilla
- 1 cup sour cream
- Confectioners' sugar for garnish (optional)

Premeasure and lay out all your ingredients on the counter. Lightly combine the flour, baking powder, baking soda and salt.

PREPARE YOUR BAKING PAN

For the most attractive appearance, use a 9-inch Bundt pan, about 4 inches deep (approximately 10-cup capacity). Or you can use a 10-inch Bundt pan (12-cup capacity) or a 10 × 4-inch round tube pan. Spray the inside of the pan with nonstick spray (PAM or something similar) or generously grease the pan with solid shortening and dust with flour, tapping out the excess flour. Be especially careful to spray or grease the Bundt pan thoroughly, including all the nooks and crannies. If greasing, a small, soft pastry brush can be very helpful. Flour the center tube by tossing a little flour on it from the tip of a teaspoon.

PREHEAT THE OVEN

Set the oven to 350 degrees. Position the rack in the center of the oven.

PREPARING THE APPLE MIXTURE (Make this first and set it aside.)

Put the diced apples, dark-brown sugar and cinnamon into a bowl and mix them together.

MIXING THE BATTER

1. In a large bowl, using a mixer, beat the butter at high speed until it is soft and smooth, about 1 minute.
2. Add the granulated sugar in two parts and continue beating, at medium speed, after each addition until the mixture is light and fluffy. Total mixing time, including scraping down the bowl with a large rubber spatula once or twice, is 4 to 5 minutes.
3. At medium speed, add the eggs one at a time, beating only until they are well blended. Remember to scrape down the bowl once or twice.
4. Add a third of the dry ingredients, all the vanilla and a third of the sour cream and mix at medium speed for about 20 seconds. Do this two more times and then beat the batter for about 1 minute until it is uniform and smooth looking. Do not overbeat.
5. Gently fold the walnuts and diced apples and any juice there is into the batter.
6. With the help of the spatula, put the batter into the baking pan. The batter should fill the pan at least to the halfway mark but no more than three-quarters full. Gently smooth the top. Drop the pan on the counter gently a couple of times to settle the batter evenly.

BAKING THE CAKE

Bake the cake 55 to 70 minutes, until the top is browned and feels springy to the touch and a cake tester or toothpick comes out clean, without any batter on it. The latter is a more important test than watching the clock.

COOLING THE CAKE

Allow the cake to cool in the pan for about 20 minutes, then turn it out onto a wire rack, right side up, to finish cooling.

SERVING THE CAKE

Before serving the cake, dust it evenly with confectioners' sugar, or you can drizzle a simple glaze over it. (See "Frostings and Glazes.")

✦ Poppy-Seed Coffee Cake ✦

Simple but elegant and a little bit European in character (the best poppy seeds come from Holland), this is a gem of a coffee cake that needs no embellishment to enhance its fine appearance and delicious taste. For special occasions, or to suit the mood of the moment, you can dust the top with a generous sprinkling of confectioners' sugar.

INGREDIENTS

          2 cups all-purpose flour
        1½ teaspoons baking powder
          ½ teaspoon baking soda
          ½ teaspoon salt
          4 ounces (1 stick) salted butter, at room temperature
          1 cup granulated sugar
          3 large eggs
          3 teaspoons lemon extract (or 2 teaspoons grated lemon peel)
          ¼ cup poppy seeds
          1 cup buttermilk

Premeasure and lay out all your ingredients on the counter. Lightly combine the flour, baking powder, baking soda and salt.

PREPARE YOUR BAKING PAN

For the most attractive appearance, use a 9-inch Bundt pan, about 4 inches deep (approximately 10-cup capacity). Or you can use a 10-inch Bundt pan (12-cup capacity) or a 10 × 4-inch round tube pan. Spray the inside of the pan with nonstick spray (PAM or something similar) or generously grease the pan with solid shortening and dust with flour, tapping out the excess flour. Be especially careful to spray or grease the Bundt pan thoroughly, including all the nooks and crannies. If greasing, a small, soft pastry brush can be very helpful. Flour the center tube by tossing a little flour on it from the tip of a teaspoon.

PREHEAT THE OVEN.

Set the oven to 350 degrees. Position the rack in the center of the oven.

MIXING THE BATTER

1. In a large bowl, using a mixer, beat the butter at high speed until it is soft and smooth, about 1 minute.
2. Add the sugar in two parts and continue beating at medium speed after each addition, until the mixture is light and fluffy. Total mixing time, including scraping down the bowl with a large rubber spatula once or twice, is about 4 to 5 minutes.
3. At medium speed, add the eggs one at a time, beating only until they are well blended. Remember to scrape down the bowl once or twice.
4. Add a third of the dry ingredients, the lemon extract or lemon peel, all the poppy seeds and a third of the buttermilk, and mix at medium speed for about 20 seconds. Do this twice more with the remaining two thirds of the dry ingredients and the buttermilk. Finally, beat the batter for about 1 minute, until it is uniform and smooth looking. Do not overbeat.
5. Pour the batter into the baking pan. The batter should fill the pan at least to the halfway mark but no more than three-quarters full. Level the top of the batter with a spatula. Drop the pan on the counter gently a couple of times to settle the batter evenly.

BAKING THE CAKE

Bake the cake 40 to 45 minutes, until the top is browned and feels springy to the touch and a cake tester or toothpick inserted into the center comes out clean, without any batter on it.

COOLING THE CAKE

Allow the cake to cool in the pan for about 20 minutes, then turn it out onto a wire rack, right side up, to finish cooling.

SERVING THE CAKE

Although it can be, and usually is, served just as it is, Poppy Seed Coffee Cake can be further enhanced by drizzling a Vanilla Glaze randomly over the top. (See "Frostings and Glazes.")

✦ Sour-Cream Coffee Cake ✦

The sour cream in this recipe helps make the cake tender and moist and also provides a special tangy note to the flavor. The addition of crushed walnuts, brown sugar and cinnamon in the filling is the final delicious touch. This cake makes an everyday coffee break into a very special one. You can serve it plain, just dusted with confectioners' sugar, or drizzle Vanilla Glaze over the cake after it has cooled.

INGREDIENTS

For the Filling

1/2 cup walnuts, in small pieces
1/3 cup dark brown sugar, firmly packed
2 teaspoons cinnamon

For the Cake

2¼ cups all-purpose flour
2 teaspoons baking powder
1/2 teaspoon baking soda
1/2 teaspoon salt
2 teaspoons vanilla
1/4 cup milk
4 ounces (1 stick) salted butter, at room temperature
1¼ cups granulated sugar
3 large eggs
1 cup sour cream
Confectioners' sugar for garnish (optional)

Premeasure and lay out all your ingredients on the counter. Lightly combine the flour, baking powder, baking soda and salt. Combine the vanilla and milk.

Prepare Your Baking Pan

For the most attractive appearance, use a 9-inch Bundt pan, about 4 inches deep (approximately 10-cup capacity). Or you can use a 10-inch Bundt pan (12-cup capacity) or a 10 × 4-inch round tube pan. Spray the inside of the pan with nonstick spray (PAM or something similar) or generously grease the pan with solid shortening and dust with flour, tapping out the excess flour. Be especially careful to spray or grease the Bundt pan thoroughly, including all the nooks and crannies. If greasing, a small, soft pastry brush can be very helpful. Flour the center tube by tossing a little flour on it from the tip of a teaspoon.

Preheat the Oven

Set the oven to 350 degrees. Position the rack in the center of the oven.

MAKING THE FILLING

Put the walnuts, dark brown sugar and cinnamon into a bowl and blend them together with a spoon or fork.

MIXING THE BATTER

1. In a large bowl, using a mixer, beat the butter at high speed until it is soft and smooth, about 1 minute.
2. Add the granulated sugar in two parts and continue beating, at medium speed, after each addition until the mixture is light and fluffy. Total mixing time, including scraping down the bowl with a large rubber spatula once or twice, is 4 to 5 minutes.
3. At medium speed, add the eggs one at a time, beating only until they are well blended. Remember to scrape down the bowl once or twice.
4. Add a third of the dry ingredients, all the vanilla-milk mixture and a third of the sour cream and mix at medium speed for about 20 seconds. Do this two more times and then beat the batter for about 1 minute or so until it is uniform and smooth looking. Do not overbeat.
5. With the help of the spatula, deposit about half of the batter into the baking pan. Using a spoon, deposit the filling in a circle over the very center of the batter. If the filling is placed on the edges, turning out the cake later on is a bit more difficult. Then deposit the rest of the batter over the filling. The batter should fill the pan at least to the halfway mark but no more than three-quarters full. Gently smooth the top. Drop the pan on the counter gently a couple of times to settle the batter evenly.

BAKING THE CAKE

Bake the cake 40 to 45 minutes, until the top is browned and feels springy to the touch and a cake tester or toothpick inserted into the center comes out clean, without any batter on it.

COOLING THE CAKE

Allow the cake to cool in the pan for about 20 minutes, then turn it out onto a wire rack, right side up, to finish cooling.

SERVING THE CAKE

Before serving the cake you can simply dust it evenly with confectioners' sugar or you can drizzle a simple glaze over it. (See "Frostings and Glazes.")

✦ Streusel Coffee Cake ✦

Streusel means "sprinkle" in German and it consists of a crumbly topping made with flour, butter, sugar and spices and, sometimes, crushed walnuts. It provides a crisp and tasty crust to whatever it is baked on, like this simple but delicious coffee cake. I opted not to use walnuts in the streusel topping but to include them, together with cinnamon and dark-brown sugar, in a center-of-the-cake filling. Not a bad idea, as you will see when you make it.

INGREDIENTS

For the Filling

1/4 cup dark brown sugar
2 teaspoons cinnamon
1/2 cup walnuts, chopped fine

For the Streusel Topping

1/4 cup dark brown sugar
3/4 cup all-purpose flour
2 teaspoons cinnamon
2 ounces (1/2 stick) salted butter, chilled

For the Cake

2 ounces (1/2 stick) salted butter, at room temperature
1/2 cup granulated sugar
1 teaspoon vanilla
2 large eggs
1 1/4 cups all-purpose flour
3/4 teaspoon baking powder
1/4 teaspoon baking soda
1/2 teaspoon salt
1/2 cup buttermilk

Premeasure and lay out all your ingredients on the counter.

PREPARE YOUR BAKING PAN

Use an 8 × 8-inch square baking pan. Spray the inside of the pan with non-stick spray (PAM or something similar) or grease the pan with solid short-ening and dust with flour, tapping out the excess flour. It would also be helpful (but not essential) to cut out a piece of parchment or wax paper the size of the pan bottom and lay it in. It makes removing the cake from the pan a bit easier.

PREHEAT THE OVEN

Set the oven to 350 degrees. Position the rack in the center of the oven.

PREPARE THE FILLING

Put the dark brown sugar, cinnamon and walnuts into a bowl and blend them together with a spoon or fork. Set this aside.

PREPARE THE STREUSEL TOPPING

Blend together the dark brown sugar, flour and cinnamon in a mixing bowl. Cut the butter into small pieces, add them to the bowl and work them into the dry mixture with your fingertips until coarse crumbs and clumps are formed. Set this aside.

MIXING THE BATTER

1. In a large bowl using a mixer, cream the butter, granulated sugar and vanilla at high speed for several minutes until the mixture is smooth and light.
2. Add the eggs and beat them in.
3. Thoroughly blend together the flour, baking powder, baking soda, and salt and add half of the mixture to the mixing bowl. Then add half the buttermilk. Beat until everything is blended together. Repeat.
4. Pour half of the batter into the baking pan and sprinkle the filling over it as evenly as you can. Then pour the other half of the batter over the filling.
5. Sprinkle the streusel topping over the batter evenly.

BAKING THE CAKE

Bake for 30 to 35 minutes until a cake tester or a toothpick inserted into the center comes out clean, without any batter on it. This is, as always, a more reliable test than watching the clock.

COOLING THE CAKE

Allow the cake to cool in the pan for about 20 minutes, then turn it out onto a wire rack, right side up, to finish cooling.

SERVING THE CAKE

Although it can be, and usually is, served just as is, Streusel Coffee Cake can be further enhanced by drizzling a Vanilla Glaze over the top. (See "Frostings and Glazes.")

✦ Banana-Nut Bread ✦

Banana breads are part of the family of baked goods called quick breads or tea breads, and, as such, they are leavened with eggs and baking powder instead of the yeast used in conventional bread baking. Even though it is called a bread, this Banana-Nut Bread is, in reality, a cake. It is a wonderful companion to morning coffee or afternoon or evening tea or, for young and old alike, a satisfying glass of cold milk. Quick and easy to prepare, it is a great way to use up those very ripe bananas in the fruit bowl. It is truly delicious.

INGREDIENTS

2 cups plus 2 tablespoons all-purpose flour
1 teaspoon baking powder
1 teaspoon baking soda
$1/2$ teaspoon salt
4 ounces (1 stick) salted butter, at room temperature
1 cup granulated sugar
3 large eggs
2 large or 3 smaller ripe bananas, crushed (1 to $1^1/2$ cups)
$1/2$ cup milk
$3/4$ cup walnuts, chopped

Premeasure and lay out all your ingredients on the counter. Lightly combine the flour, baking powder, baking soda and salt.

PREPARE YOUR BAKING PAN

Use one 9 × 5 × 3-inch or $8^1/2$ × $4^1/2$ × $2^1/2$-inch loaf pan. Spray the inside of the pan with nonstick spray (PAM or something similar) or grease the pan with solid shortening and dust with flour, tapping out the excess flour. It would also be helpful (but not essential) to cut out a piece of parchment or wax paper the size of the pan bottom and lay it in. It makes removing the cake from the pan a bit easier.

PREHEAT THE OVEN

Set the oven to 350 degrees. Position the rack in the center of the oven.

MIXING THE BATTER

1. In a large bowl, using a mixer, beat the butter at high speed until it is soft and smooth, about 1 minute.
2. Add the sugar in two parts and continue beating after each addition, at medium speed, until the mixture is light and fluffy. Total mixing time, including scraping down the bowl with a large rubber spatula once or twice, is 4 to 5 minutes.
3. At medium speed, add the eggs one at a time, beating only until well blended. Remember to scrape down the bowl once or twice.
4. Add the dry ingredients and beat until the mixture is smooth.
5. Add the crushed bananas and milk and mix just until incorporated.
6. Add the chopped walnuts and lightly mix them in.
7. Pour the batter into the baking pan and level the top with a spatula or spoon. Fill the pan about three-quarters full. If there is any excess batter you can use it to make cupcakes.

BAKING THE CAKE

Bake for 55 to 60 minutes until the top is browned and feels springy to the touch and a cake tester or toothpick comes out clean, without any batter on it.

COOLING THE CAKE

Allow the cake to cool in the pan for about 20 minutes, then turn it out onto a wire rack, right side up, to finish cooling.

✦ Cranberry Bread ✦

When cranberry bread is made with fresh cranberries it is a wonderful autumn treat, with red berries showing through like jewels. It is also delicious made with dried cranberries, so you needn't be restricted to just one season of the year. The orange juice and grated orange peel add the perfect flavor note.

INGREDIENTS

- 1³/₄ **cups all-purpose flour**
- 1 **teaspoon baking powder**
- ¹/₄ **teaspoon baking soda**
- ¹/₂ **teaspoon salt**
- ¹/₂ **cup vegetable oil (canola or safflower)**
- 1 **cup granulated sugar**
- 2 **large eggs**
- ¹/₄ **cup orange juice**
- 1 **teaspoon vanilla**
- 1 **teaspoon grated orange peel**
- 1¹/₂ **cups cranberries, fresh or dried (if dried, add 2 additional tablespoons of orange juice)**
- ³/₄ **cup walnuts, in small pieces**

Premeasure and lay out all your ingredients on the counter. Lightly combine the flour, baking powder, baking soda and salt.

PREPARE YOUR BAKING PAN

Use one 9 × 5 × 3-inch or 8¹/₂ × 4¹/₂ × 2¹/₂-inch loaf pan. Spray the inside of the pan with nonstick spray (PAM or something similar) or grease the pan with solid shortening and dust with flour, tapping out the excess flour. It would also be helpful (but not essential) to cut out a piece of parchment or wax paper the size of the pan bottom and lay it in. It makes removing the cake from the pan a bit easier.

PREHEAT THE OVEN

Set the oven to 350 degrees. Position the rack in the center of the oven.

MIXING THE BATTER

1. In a large bowl, using a mixer, beat the oil, sugar, eggs, orange juice, vanilla and grated orange peel until the mixture is smooth, about 1 minute.
2. Add the dry ingredients and beat until the mixture is smooth.
3. Add the cranberries and walnuts and gently mix them in at low speed until they are evenly distributed.
4. Pour the batter into the loaf pan. The batter should fill the pan at least to the halfway mark but no more than three-quarters full.

BAKING THE CAKE

Bake for 60 to 70 minutes until the top is browned and feels springy to the touch and a cake tester or toothpick comes out clean, without any batter on it.

COOLING THE CAKE

Allow the cake to cool in the pan for about 20 minutes, then turn it out onto a wire rack, right side up, to finish cooling.

✦ Date-Nut Bread ✦

Dates are a staple food of the Eastern Mediterranean and they are a nutritional delight—high in fiber and also sodium and fat free. Fortunately, they are delicious and as sweet as sugar and, when blended together with the other ingredients in this recipe, they make a great-tasting tea bread. If you have any cream cheese in the refrigerator, try a cream-cheese sandwich on date-nut bread and see if you can stop at just one.

INGREDIENTS

    2 cups all-purpose flour
    1 teaspoon baking powder
  1/2 teaspoon baking soda
  1/2 teaspoon salt
  1/2 teaspoon cinnamon
  1/4 teaspoon allspice
 13/4 cups chopped dates (one 8-ounce box)
  3/4 cup boiling water
    2 ounces (1/2 stick) salted butter, at room temperature
    1 teaspoon vanilla
  3/4 cup dark brown sugar
    2 large eggs
    1 cup buttermilk
  3/4 cup walnuts, in small pieces

Premeasure and lay out all your ingredients on the counter. Lightly combine the flour, baking powder, baking soda, salt, cinnamon and allspice.

PREPARE YOUR BAKING PAN

Use one 9 × 5 × 3-inch or 8½ × 4½ × 2½-inch loaf pan. Spray the inside of the pan with nonstick spray (PAM or something similar) or grease the pan with solid shortening and dust with flour, tapping out the excess flour. It would also be helpful (but not essential) to cut out a piece of parchment or wax paper the size of the pan bottom and lay it in. It makes removing the cake from the pan a bit easier.

PREHEAT THE OVEN

Set the oven to 350 degrees. Position the rack in the center of the oven.

MIXING THE BATTER

1. Put the dates in a small bowl and pour the boiling water over them. Put aside for 15 minutes before using them.
2. In a large bowl, using a mixer, beat the butter, vanilla and the sugar at high speed until the mixture is soft and smooth, about 1 minute.
3. At medium speed, add the eggs one at a time, beating only until well blended. Remember to scrape down the bowl.
4. Add one half of the dry ingredients and one half of the buttermilk and beat only until the mixture is smooth. Repeat with the other half.
5. Blend in the dates and water.
6. Lightly mix in the walnuts.
7. Pour the batter into the baking pan. The batter should fill the pan at least to the halfway mark but no more than three-quarters full. Level the top of the batter with a spatula or spoon.

Baking the Cake

Bake for 65 to 75 minutes until the top is browned and feels springy to the touch and a cake tester or toothpick inserted into the center comes out clean, without any batter on it.

Cooling the Cake

Allow the cake to cool in the pan for about 20 minutes, then turn it out onto a wire rack, right side up, to finish cooling.

✦ Pumpkin Bread ✦

This is another great addition to the quick-bread, tea-bread family and one that should definitely be part of your baking repertoire. The wonderful aroma itself is worth the effort of making it. If you enjoy pumpkin pie you will really love this delicious pumpkin bread.

INGREDIENTS

1¼	cups all-purpose flour
1½	teaspoons baking powder
¼	teaspoon baking soda
½	teaspoon salt
1	teaspoon cinnamon
⅛	teaspoon nutmeg
¼	teaspoon ginger
⅛	teaspoon allspice
¼	cup vegetable oil (canola or safflower)
1	cup granulated sugar
1	large egg
1	cup pumpkin puree (canned solid-pack, not pumpkin-pie mix)
¾	cup walnuts, in small pieces

Premeasure and lay out all your ingredients on the counter. Lightly combine the flour, baking powder, baking soda, salt, cinnamon, nutmeg, ginger and allspice.

PREPARE YOUR BAKING PAN

Use an 8½ × 4½ × 2½-inch loaf pan. Spray the inside of the pan with nonstick spray (PAM or something similar) or grease the pan with solid shortening and dust with flour, tapping out the excess flour. It would also be helpful (but not essential) to cut out a piece of parchment or wax paper the size of the pan bottom and lay it in. It makes removing the cake from the pan a bit easier.

PREHEAT THE OVEN

Set the oven to 350 degrees. Position the rack in the center of the oven.

MIXING THE BATTER

1. In a large bowl, using a mixer, beat the vegetable oil, sugar and egg at high speed until the mixture is smooth, about 1 minute.
2. Add the pumpkin and mix until the mixture is uniform in appearance.
3. Add the dry ingredients and beat only until mixture is smooth.
4. Lightly mix in the walnuts.
5. Pour the batter into the baking pan and level the top with a spatula or spoon. The batter should fill the pan at least to the halfway mark but no more than three-quarters full. If you want to use up the entire can of pumpkin, which contains approximately 2 cups, just double the recipe and make two loaves or one large loaf plus some cupcakes. Pumpkin bread freezes beautifully.

BAKING THE CAKE

Bake for 55 to 65 minutes until the top is browned and feels springy to the touch and a cake tester or toothpick comes out clean, without any batter on it.

COOLING THE CAKE

Allow the cake to cool in the pan for about 20 minutes, then turn it out onto a wire rack, right side up, to finish cooling.

✦ Zucchini Bread ✦

You would have to be a clairvoyant to know that zucchini is the vegetable used in this quick bread. You won't taste the zucchini at all but you will know that the result is moist, flavorful and delicious and that you're happy you made it.

INGREDIENTS

$1\frac{1}{2}$ cups all-purpose flour
$\frac{1}{2}$ teaspoon baking powder
$\frac{1}{2}$ teaspoon baking soda
$\frac{1}{2}$ teaspoon salt
$\frac{1}{2}$ teaspoon cinnamon
1 zucchini (about $\frac{1}{2}$ pound)
$\frac{1}{2}$ cup vegetable oil (canola or safflower)
2 large eggs
1 cup granulated sugar
1 teaspoon vanilla
$\frac{3}{4}$ cup walnuts, in small or medium pieces

Premeasure and lay out all your ingredients on the counter. Lightly combine the flour, baking powder, baking soda, salt and cinnamon.

PREPARE YOUR BAKING PAN

Use one $9 \times 5 \times 3$-inch or $8\frac{1}{2} \times 4\frac{1}{2} \times 2\frac{1}{2}$-inch loaf pan. Spray the inside of the pan with nonstick spray (PAM or something similar) or grease the pan with solid shortening and dust with flour, tapping out the excess flour. It would also be helpful (but not essential) to cut out a piece of parchment or

wax paper the size of the pan bottom and lay it in. It makes removing the cake from the pan a bit easier.

PREHEAT THE OVEN

Set the oven to 350 degrees. Position the rack in the center of the oven.

MIXING THE BATTER

1. Wash the zucchini and trim the ends off but leave the skin on. Grate it on the larger holes of a hand-held grater or with the shredder blade of a food processor. You are aiming for very small slivers or pieces of zucchini, not zucchini mush. Set it aside.
2. In a large bowl, using a mixer, beat together the oil, eggs, sugar and vanilla for a minute or so.
3. Add the dry ingredients and mix everything together at low speed until the batter is uniform.
4. Add the zucchini and gently mix it in.
5. Mix in the walnuts.
6. Pour the batter into the waiting loaf pan. The batter should fill the pan at least to the halfway mark but no more than three-quarters full.

BAKING THE CAKE

Bake for about 1 hour, until the top feels springy to the touch and a cake tester or toothpick inserted into the center of the cake comes out clean, without any batter on it.

COOLING THE CAKE

Allow the cake to cool in the pan for about 20 minutes, then turn it out onto a wire rack, right side up, to finish cooling.

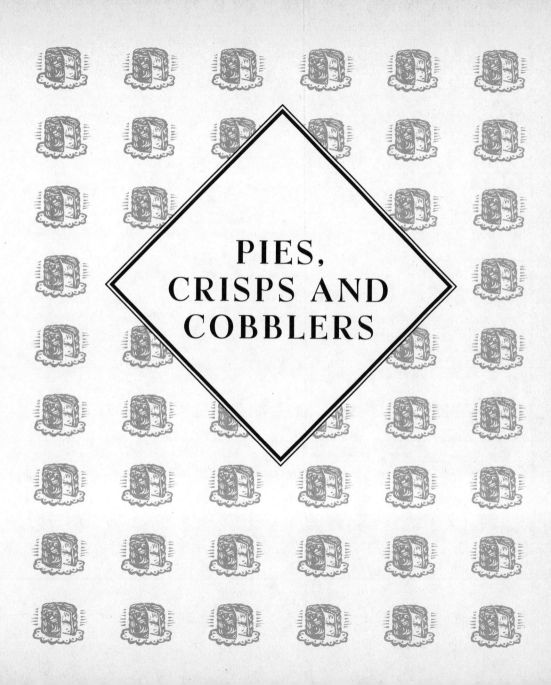

PIES, CRISPS AND COBBLERS

✦ Perfect Pastry Dough ✦

The happy decision to make a pecan, apple, lemon meringue or cherry pie should not be shadowed by the fear of not being able to make a good enough pastry crust. It is a fundamental skill that every baker should have, and yet many don't. It is for this reason that I have settled for just one single recipe for a pastry dough that is quick and easy to make and results in an absolutely delicious crust every single time. To me, it seems better to be able to do this one crust successfully (with my eyes practically closed because I've done it so many times) than to experiment endlessly with a dozen different recipes. Quick, easy, foolproof and delicious is a hard combination to beat.

MASTER DOUGH RECIPE

For a One-Crust Pie

- 1½ cups all-purpose flour
- ¼ teaspoon salt
- 2 tablespoons granulated sugar
- 4 ounces (1 stick) salted butter, chilled
- 1 large egg yolk
- 4 tablespoons (¼ cup) ice water

For a Two-Crust Pie

3 **cups all-purpose flour**
1/2 **teaspoon salt**
4 **tablespoons (1/4 cup) granulated sugar**
8 **ounces (2 sticks) salted butter, chilled**
2 **large egg yolks**
8 **tablespoons (1/2 cup) ice water**

MIXING THE DOUGH USING THE FOOD PROCESSOR

Put the flour, salt and sugar into the work bowl fitted with the steel blade and pulse for a few seconds to get them thoroughly mixed together. Put the cold butter on a plate, slice it into smaller pieces and place the pieces fairly evenly in a circle on top of the dry ingredients. Pulse just until the mixture looks coarse and mealy. Be careful not to pulse too long or too much. When you lift off the cover and feel it with your fingers, it will feel uniformly mealy but if you see or feel a few pea-sized pieces of butter interspersed in the mixture, that's just fine. Let them be. Now you're ready for the second step.

Lightly mix together the egg yolk (or yolks, if you are making a two-crust pie) and the ice water in a cup, pour this over the flour-butter mixture and turn on the machine. As soon as the mixture starts to clump up to form a dough, stop the machine immediately. It is important not to overmix the dough, as this "develops" the gluten and toughens the eventual crust. Take the dough out of the food processor and place it in another bowl or on the counter and push it gently together to form a ball. Feel the dough with your fingers. If it presses together easily, you are done. On the other hand, if it still feels a little too dry and crumbly, then add another *teaspoon* of ice water and gently work it in. If you have to add still another teaspoon of water, that's all right. Just never add more than 1 teaspoon at a time. The final dough should feel damp and pliable and the pieces should adhere easily to each other when you press them together, but you don't want the dough really wet. I usually find it unnecessary to add the additional teaspoonfuls of water.

Spread a good-sized piece of plastic wrap on the counter, gather up the dough into a ball (or two balls if you are making two crusts), place the dough in the center, wrap it up and flatten the ball into a thick, round, flat disk. This will make rolling it out easier when you are ready to do so. Put the dough in the refrigerator—it should be chilled before you use it. If you plan to use it as soon as possible, let it remain in the refrigerator for about 30 minutes. On the other hand, if you want to use it at another time, you can keep it in the refrigerator for a few days without harm. When you do take it out, however, make sure you let it remain out at room temperature long enough so that it becomes pliable. Working with a very cold dough that breaks up as you try to roll it out is not a rewarding experience.

Mixing the Dough by Hand

Put the flour, salt and sugar into a large bowl and stir them together. Cut the butter into about eight pieces and add them to the dry ingredients. Using your fingertips, pinch and rub the butter into the flour until the entire mixture looks uniformly coarse and mealy. An occasional pea-sized piece of coated butter is all right. You can also do the above by using two knives or, better still, a small, crescent-shaped hand-held pastry cutter. Break the egg yolk (or yolks) into a cup, add the ice water, stir them together and add this mixture to the bowl. Quickly start stirring with a strong fork until the dough is evenly moistened and starts to hold together. If it still seems a bit dry and crumbly, add another teaspoonful of water, or even two if necessary. Do not add water generously. The least amount of water, the better. When the dough adheres together, gather it into a ball (or two balls, if you're making two crusts), wrap it in plastic wrap and gently flatten the ball of dough into a thick, round, flat disk and place it in the refrigerator for about 30 minutes before you take it out to use. On the other hand, if you want to use it at a later time, you can keep it in the refrigerator for a few days without harm. When you do take it out, however, make sure you let it remain out at room temperature long enough so that it becomes soft and pliable.

Mixing the Dough with the Electric Mixer

Follow the same basic instructions as described above for the food processor, using the beaters at low speed to break up the butter and form the mealy mixture. Add the yolk and ice water mixture and form the dough with the beaters, adding a teaspoonful or two of additional water if necessary. When the dough is formed, stop the mixer immediately so as not to overmix the dough. Follow the same instructions as above to wrap and refrigerate the dough.

Note on Refrigerating and Freezing the Dough

If the dough is carefully double-wrapped in plastic wrap, it may safely be kept in the refrigerator for several days. Just be sure to let it become pliable and workable at room temperature before you start to roll it out. It should still be cool, however, and not warm. Double-wrapped, it may also be safely kept in the freezer for a couple of months. When you are ready to use it, however, defrost it overnight in the refrigerator first.

ROLLING OUT THE PASTRY DOUGH

For Both Single-Crust and Double-Crust Pies

Use a smooth, flat and, of course, large enough surface for rolling out the dough. A marble slab would be a gift from heaven but, lacking that, wood, formica or stainless steel are just fine. Put some flour in a small dish next to the surface you will be working on, and also a thin, flexible spatula, a small, sharp knife and a pair of scissors. You can use a simple, solid, one-piece rolling pin or a large ball-bearing one, which is what I use. Either one will do a good job.

Lightly scatter a little flour on your surface, place the disk of dough on it, and then immediately turn it over so that there is a little flour on both sides. Holding the rolling pin in one hand, pound the dough with it fairly gently inch by inch from one end of the disk to the other. Turn it over, rotate it half a turn and repeat the pounding. The pounding helps make the dough more elastic and manageable. As you work with the dough (turning it over, rolling it, etc.) you will need small dustings of flour to prevent the dough from sticking. You may have to do this fairly often so get into the habit of using very small amounts of flour each time. Although you do need the flour to prevent sticking, the less you use the better the crust will be.

Now start rolling out the dough, starting from the center and working toward the edges. Try not to roll over the edges of the dough too much, as it thins out the dough there and makes it sticky. Stop rolling just before you reach the edge or lighten up on the pressure if you do go over it. Keep rotating the dough halfway around as you roll it out, to maintain the circle. Do this on both sides, using a little flour when it is necessary to prevent sticking. If you have a tear in the dough, just push the dough together with your fingers to mend it. If it does need a little help to stick together, just dampen the edges before you push them together. The dough should be rolled out to about ⅛-inch thickness.

Making the Bottom Crust of a Single-Crust Pie

1. When you have rolled out the dough to a fairly large, round circle, turn the pie plate upside down and place it over the center of the dough. You will need about 2 inches of excess dough around the entire rim of the upside-down pie plate. Trim the excess away with the tip of the knife.

2. Remove the pie plate and turn it right side up. Lay the rolling pin on the edge of the dough and roll the dough around the rolling pin so that it can be carried over to the pie plate, centered over it and then deposited on it. If you need a little help in getting the dough started onto the rolling pin, just slide the spatula under the edge of the dough to loosen it.

3. Now fit the dough into the pie plate, trying not to stretch it. Run your fingers gently over the dough, smoothing it over the bottom and up the sides. Any excess of dough over the rim should be turned under in order to build up the edge. Using the fingers of both hands, keep on evening out and pressing together the dough on the rim so that this top edge ends up fairly uniform in appearance.

4. At this point you are ready to make this top edge decorative. You can flute the edge as shown in the illustration on the next page.

5. When you are satisfied with the thing of beauty that you have created, put it into the refrigerator to let the gluten relax and the dough cool down. This helps to prevent shrinking of the crust during the baking. If you intend to proceed with baking the crust as soon as possible, then a 20- or 30-minute rest in the refrigerator will be sufficient. You could keep it there for a couple of hours if you wanted to or, well wrapped in plastic wrap, even for a couple of days. Double-wrapped, you could keep it in the

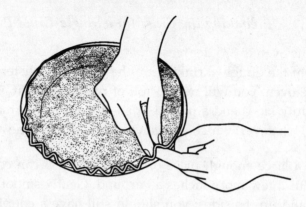

freezer for a couple of months and then defrost it in the refrigerator the day before you intend to use it.

PREBAKING YOUR PASTRY CRUST

Or, Why I Prebake the Bottom Crusts of All Single-Crust Pies

Nothing is more off-putting than sitting down to a luscious-looking pie or tart and finding out, after the first bite, that the bottom crust is soggy, under-baked and tasteless. You will probably continue eating it, but the bloom is off the rose, and a lot of the enjoyment will be gone. A wet filling poured into a raw pie crust almost invariably results in a soggy bottom crust. The only way to overcome this problem is to prebake or partially prebake the crust before you pour in the filling and put the pie into the oven.

I usually find it useful to make several prebaked pie crusts at the same time and put the extra ones in the freezer for future use. Well wrapped in plastic wrap and then enclosed in a plastic bag, they will last in your freezer for months. Simply defrost the crust for an hour or use it frozen.

Prebaking the Crust for a Single-Crust Pie

Preheat the oven to 375 degrees.

To prevent the dough shrinking on the sides and blistering on the bottom while in the oven, you will need a roll of regular-weight aluminum foil (not the heavy-duty kind) and a pound or so of dry beans (great northern beans, navy beans, whatever) which you can reuse time and time again.

1. Cut off a large enough piece of foil so that you can cover the entire pie plate plus a few more inches all around. Gently smooth the foil over the dough and up the sides; you should still have a couple of inches of foil sticking up above the rim. This extra foil will make removing the beans easier.

2. Pour the beans into the aluminum foil, smooth the top so that the beans are level with the rim and place the pie plate in the oven. The weight of the beans will help keep the dough intact in the pie plate.

3. Bake the crust for about 30 minutes to allow the dough to dry out and set up and to allow the edges of the crust to start to take on some color. If the bottom of the crust is still wet and raw-looking after you lift up the foil and remove the beans, you will have a little more trouble in the second baking, the one without the beans. In this case it would be advisable to replace the aluminum foil and the beans and continue the baking for another 5 or 10 minutes or so. After this is done, remove the pie plate to the counter. Remove the beans and save them for next time.

Reduce the oven temperature to 350 degrees.

4. Put the crust back in the oven to continue baking, without the beans this time. Check it in about 5 minutes to make sure the hot air under the

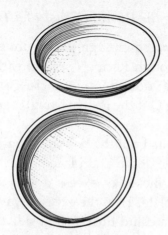

bottom of the crust is not ballooning it up. If it is, use the tip of a sharp knife to puncture the balloon and let the hot air escape. If it still does not lay down flat, push it down gently with the bottom of a small saucepan.

5. From the time you put the crust back into the 350-degree oven, it should take anywhere from 8 to 15 minutes to finish baking to a light brown or amber color. You have to watch it like a hawk, though, because it can overbake very quickly. Look into the oven often and, the moment the edges of the crust are a light brown and the bottom looks done, snatch the plate from the oven and put it on a wire rack to cool down. The crust continues to bake for a bit longer after you remove it from the oven—that is the reason for removing it quickly.

Making the Bottom Crust of a Two-Crust Pie

After you have prepared enough pastry dough for a two-crust pie by following the "Master Dough Recipe" printed earlier in this chapter, divide it evenly so that you have dough for a top crust and a bottom crust. Now read the section on "Rolling Out the Pastry Dough" printed earlier in this chapter.

1. When you have rolled out the bottom dough to a large, round circle, turn the pie plate upside down and place it over the center of the dough. You will need about 3 inches of excess dough around the entire rim of the upside-down pie plate. Trim the excess away with the tip of the knife.
2. Remove the pie plate and turn it right side up. Lay the rolling pin on the edge of the dough and roll the dough around the rolling pin so that it can be carried over to the pie plate, centered over it and then deposited on it. If you need a little help in getting the dough started onto the rolling pin, just use the spatula under the edge of the dough to loosen it.
3. Now fit the dough into the plate, trying not to stretch it. Run your fingers gently over the dough, smoothing it over the bottom and up the sides. Any excess of dough rising above the top of the plate should be turned under in order to build up the edge. Using the fingers of both hands, keep on evening out the dough on the rim so that this top edge ends up fairly uniform in appearance.
4. Do *not* prebake the bottom crust of a two-crust pie.

Covering a Two-Crust Pie with the Top Dough

1. After filling the bottom crust, roll out the dough for the top crust. Trim the edges so that you have a circle that will cover the top of the pie plate with at least 1 inch of extra dough all around.

2. Brush the edges of the bottom pastry with water.
3. Gently ease the dough for the top onto the bottom. Turn the edges of the top pastry under the edges of the bottom pastry. Press to seal. Flute the edge decoratively.
4. Place the pie in the refrigerator for at least 20 minutes before baking if time permits.
5. Brush the top with a mixture of 1 egg and $1/4$ cup of milk but don't leave puddles on the dough. Sprinkle a small amount of sugar evenly across the top.
6. Cut three or four vents in the top of the pie to release the steam while it is baking. Make several small circles or triangles or $1/8$-inch-wide slits.

✦ Apple Pie ✦

Apple pie is as necessary in the American home as Mom in the kitchen and the Stars and Stripes hanging on the front porch. Made with fresh crisp apples, flavored only with cinnamon and lemon juice, and served with (or without) a slice of cheddar cheese or a scoop of vanilla ice cream, it is the quintessential American dessert.

INGREDIENTS

Choose slightly tart cooking apples such as Granny Smith, Gravenstein, Baldwin, Pippin, Northern Spy, or even Golden Delicious, which is not particularly tart but holds its shape well in baking.

Pastry dough for a two-crust pie (see page 101)

For The Filling

- 3/4 cup dark brown sugar, firmly packed (or 1/2 cup if apples are Golden Delicious)
- 3 tablespoons all-purpose flour
- 1 teaspoon cinnamon
- 7 medium-size apples (to make about 7 cups sliced), peeled and cored and placed in a bowl of cold water
- 1 teaspoon lemon juice (or 1 1/2 teaspoons if apples are Golden Delicious)
- 2 tablespoons salted butter, chilled

For the Glaze

- 1 large egg
- 1/4 cup milk
- 1 to 2 tablespoons granulated sugar

PREPARE THE BOTTOM CRUST

Roll out the dough for the bottom crust to about ⅛-inch thickness. Set a 9-inch pie plate upside down over the pastry; trim with a sharp knife so that you have a circle approximately 3 inches larger than the outside rim of the plate. Gently ease the dough into the plate, smoothing it down along the entire bottom and up the sides and leaving the excess hanging over the top edge. You won't be using up all of the dough so put aside the excess. You can make little cookies with it if you like. Put the pie plate in the refrigerator.

PREHEAT THE OVEN

Set the oven to 425 degrees. Position the rack in the lower part of the oven and place a cookie sheet on the rack.

PREPARING THE FILLING

1. Put the sugar, flour and cinnamon into a large bowl and mix them together.
2. Slice the apples thinly, add them and the lemon juice to the brown-sugar mixture and toss until they are coated evenly.
3. Heap and press the apples into the pastry shell.
4. Cut the cold butter into bits and scatter it evenly over the apples. Set aside.

PREPARE THE TOP CRUST

1. Roll out the dough for the top crust. Trim the edges so that you have a circle that will cover the top of the filled pie plate with at least 1 inch extra dough all around.
2. Brush the edges of the bottom pastry with water.
3. Gently ease the top pastry onto the bottom. Turn the edges of the top pastry under the edges of the bottom pastry and press to seal. Flute the edge decoratively, if you like.
4. Place the pie in the refrigerator for at least 20 minutes before baking if time permits.
5. Just before baking brush the top crust with a mixture of the egg and milk but don't leave puddles on the dough. Sprinkle a small amount of sugar evenly across the top.
6. Cut three or four vents in the top of the pie to release the steam while baking. Make several small circles or triangles or 1/8-inch-wide slits.

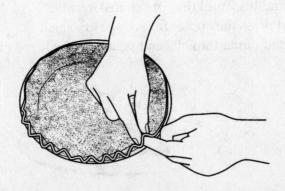

BAKING THE PIE

Bake on the cookie sheet at 425 degrees for 20 minutes; reduce heat to 350° and bake approximately 60 to 80 minutes longer or until the crust is nicely browned and the apples are tender when pierced with a fork or knife. It is better to overbake a little than underbake. If the crust starts to get too brown, just cover the pie with a large piece of aluminum foil. The length of the baking time is dependent on the thickness of the crust and the sliced apples.

COOLING THE PIE

Let the pie cool on a wire rack. As the pie cools, some of the liquid will be reabsorbed.

SERVING THE PIE

Serve slightly warm or at room temperature or right from the refrigerator, as the occasion warrants. The pie can be served with a thin slice of sharp cheddar cheese, a scoop of vanilla ice cream or a dollop of whipped cream or all by its wonderful self.

✦ Cherry Pie ✦

Cherry pie is another dessert that brings a smile of anticipation to everyone's face when it is brought to the table. Although it would be nice if fresh, tart red cherries were available all year round, unfortunately they are not and so I have provided a recipe using canned tart red cherries which are always available. Because they are simply packed in water, without added sugar or thickeners, they make a delicious cherry pie so don't hesitate to use them. Serve it with vanilla ice cream, of course.

INGREDIENTS

Pastry dough for a two-crust 9-inch pie (see page 101)

For the Filling

1 cup granulated sugar
3 tablespoons cornstarch
4 cups (two 16-ounce cans) pitted tart cherries, canned and packed in water, drained (reserve $1/3$ cup of the juice; don't use cherry pie filling)
1 teaspoon lemon juice
2 tablespoons salted butter

For the Glaze

1 large egg
1/4 cup milk
1 to 2 teaspoons granulated sugar

PREPARE THE BOTTOM CRUST

Roll out the dough for the bottom crust to about $1/8$-inch thickness. Set a 9-inch pie plate upside down over the pastry; trim with a sharp knife so that you have a circle approximately 3 inches larger than the outside rim of the plate.

Gently ease the dough into the plate, smoothing it down along the entire bottom and up the sides and leaving the excess hanging over the top edge. Put the pie plate in the refrigerator.

PREHEAT THE OVEN

Set the oven to 425 degrees. Position the rack in the lower part of the oven and place a cookie sheet on the rack.

PREPARING THE FILLING

1. Put the sugar and cornstarch into a large bowl and mix them together.
2. Add the reserved cherry juice, the lemon juice and the drained cherries to the large bowl and stir this mixture until the cherries are evenly coated.
3. Pour the mixture into the waiting pastry shell and smooth it out evenly.
4. Cut the cold butter into bits and scatter it evenly over the cherries. Set aside.

PREPARE THE TOP CRUST

1. Roll out the dough for the top crust. Trim the edges so that you have a circle that will cover the top of the filled pie plate with at least 1 inch extra dough all around.
2. Brush the edges of the bottom pastry with water.
3. Gently ease the top pastry onto the bottom crust. Turn the edges of the top pastry under the edges of the bottom pastry and push the joined dough back over the top edge of the pie plate. Press to seal. With a sharp knife, cut off any excess dough extending past the top edge. Flute the edge decoratively, if you like.
4. Place the pie in the refrigerator for at least 20 minutes before baking if time permits.

5. Just before baking brush the top crust with a mixture of the egg and milk but don't leave puddles on the dough. Sprinkle a small amount of sugar evenly across the top.
6. Cut three or four vents in the top of the pie to release the steam while baking. Make several small circles or triangles or ⅛-inch-wide slits.

BAKING THE PIE

Bake on the cookie sheet at 425 degrees for 20 minutes, reduce heat to 350 degrees and bake approximately 50 to 60 minutes longer or until the crust is nicely browned. It is better to overbake a little than underbake. If the crust starts to get too brown, just cover the pie with a large piece of aluminum foil.

COOLING THE PIE

Let the pie cool on a wire rack. As the pie cools, some of the liquid will be reabsorbed.

SERVING THE PIE

Serve slightly warm or at room temperature. The pie can be served with a scoop of vanilla ice cream or a dollop of whipped cream or just the way it is—a piece of perfect cherry pie.

✦ Banana Cream Pie ✦

A creamy, vanilla-flavored custard poured over ripe banana slices in an all-butter pastry crust and heaped with whipped cream attracts lots of attention. This one is easy to make and is the perfect antidote for people who think they don't like cream pie.

INGREDIENTS

1 prebaked 9-inch pie crust (see page 108)

For the Filling

2 cups half-and-half (or 1½ cups milk plus ½ cup whipping cream)
½ cup plus 2 tablespoons granulated sugar
3 tablespoons cornstarch
¼ teaspoon salt
3 large egg yolks
2 teaspoons vanilla
2 large ripe bananas

For the Whipped-Cream Topping

1 cup heavy whipping cream
2 tablespoons confectioners' sugar
½ teaspoon vanilla

MIXING THE FILLING

1. Put the half-and-half into a saucepan.

2. Stir together thoroughly, in a bowl, the sugar, cornstarch and salt. Add this mixture to the saucepan, stirring everything together until all the lumps are gone.

3. Lightly beat the egg yolks and add them to the saucepan, together with the vanilla.

4. Cook the mixture over medium heat, stirring from time to time while it is heating. When the mixture starts to get hot, stir continuously to prevent sticking.

5. The mixture will start to thicken as it gets hotter and reaches a slow boil. Let it quietly boil (keep stirring) for about 1 minute and then immediately remove it from the heat. If it starts to boil too strongly during the last minute of boiling, just lift the saucepan a little above the heat while continuing to stir. Cool the filling for about 10 minutes.

6. Slice one of the bananas thinly and evenly into the waiting pie crust and then pour in half the hot filling. Slice the other banana over the filling and pour in the rest of the hot filling. Even the top out with a spatula if necessary.

7. After cooling, place the pie in refrigerator to chill thoroughly, about 1 hour. After the pie has been chilled, cover the filling with sweetened whipped cream and replace it in the refrigerator until ready to serve.

MAKING THE SWEETENED WHIPPED CREAM

1. Use heavy whipping cream instead of plain whipping cream as it has a higher butterfat content and will make a firmer whipped cream.

2. Make sure that the bowl (preferably metal, and not too large) and the beaters, or whisk, that you will be using are cold. Put them in the freezer for a few minutes, or in the refrigerator for 10 to 15 minutes before you start the process. Also make sure that the cream is well chilled.

3. Start mixing the cream at medium speed (in order to prevent splashing) and then increase to high speed after it has thickened a little.
4. When soft peaks are just starting to form, add the confectioners' sugar and vanilla and continue beating until the whipped cream is firm. Do not overbeat.

Variation

Vanilla Cream Pie
Eliminate the bananas. Add an additional teaspoon of vanilla to the filling and pour the filling into the waiting pie crust. Chill and cover with sweetened whipped cream as above.

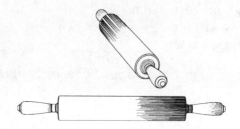

✦ Chocolate Cream Pie ✦

There is something luscious in just thinking about a slice of chocolate cream pie. A tender butter crust supporting a rich, quivering chocolate filling topped with a mound of sweetened whipped cream is as sensual a vision as anyone could hope to see. The fact that it is also very, very delicious completes the picture. Happily, with this recipe, it is also easy to make.

INGREDIENTS

1 prebaked 9-inch pie crust (see page 108)

For the Filling

2 cups half-and-half (or 1½ cups milk plus ½ cup whipping cream)
2½ ounces (2½ squares) unsweetened chocolate
1 cup granulated sugar
2½ tablespoons cornstarch
¼ teaspoon salt
2 large eggs, beaten

For the Whipped Cream Topping

1 cup heavy whipping cream
2 tablespoons confectioners' sugar
½ teaspoon vanilla

MIXING THE FILLING

1. Put the half-and-half and the chocolate into a heavy-bottomed saucepan and cook over medium heat, stirring occasionally, until the chocolate is melted.

2. Stir together thoroughly, in a bowl, the sugar, cornstarch and salt. Add this mixture to the saucepan, stirring everything together until all the lumps are gone.

3. Stir a little of the hot mixture into the beaten eggs and then pour it all back into the saucepan.

4. Continue cooking this mixture over medium heat, stirring from time to time. When the mixture starts to get hot, stir continuously.

5. The mixture will start to thicken as it gets hotter and reaches a slow boil. Let it quietly boil (keep stirring) for about 1 minute and then immediately remove it from the heat. If it starts to boil too strongly during the last minute of boiling, just lift the saucepan a little above the heat while continuing to stir.

6. Pour the hot filling into the waiting pie crust. Even the top out with a spatula, if necessary.

7. After cooling, place the pie in the refrigerator to chill thoroughly.

8. After the pie has been chilled, cover the filling with sweetened whipped cream and replace it in the refrigerator until ready to serve.

MAKING THE SWEETENED WHIPPED CREAM

1. Use heavy whipping cream instead of plain whipping cream as it has a higher butterfat content and will make a firmer whipped cream.

2. Make sure that the bowl (preferably metal, and not too large) and the beaters, or whisk, that you will be using are cold. Put them in the freezer for a few minutes, or in the refrigerator for 10 to 15 minutes before you start the process. Also make sure that the cream is well chilled.

3. Start mixing the cream at medium speed (in order to prevent splashing) and then at high speed after it has thickened a little.

4. When soft peaks are just starting to form, add the confectioners' sugar and vanilla and continue beating until the whipped cream is firm. Do not overbeat.

✦ Coconut Cream Pie ✦

Another rich and unctuous member of the family of cream pies. This time it is coconut that plays the starring role and is deserving of all the applause. The pie is smooth, creamy and coconutty—a winning combination.

INGREDIENTS

    1 prebaked 9-inch pie crust (see page 108)

For the Filling

    2 cups half-and-half (or 1½ cups milk plus ½ cup whipping cream)
  ½ cup plus 2 tablespoons granulated sugar
    3 tablespoons cornstarch
  ¼ teaspoon salt
    3 large egg yolks
    2 teaspoons vanilla
1½ cups sweetened flaked coconut

For the Whipped Cream Topping

    1 cup heavy whipping cream
    2 tablespoons confectioners' sugar
  ½ teaspoon vanilla

MIXING THE FILLING

1. Put the half-and-half into a saucepan.
2. Stir together thoroughly, in a bowl, the sugar, cornstarch and salt. Add

this mixture to the saucepan, stirring everything together until all the lumps are gone.

3. Lightly beat the egg yolks and add to the saucepan, together with the vanilla.

4. Cook this mixture over medium heat, stirring from time to time while the mixture is heating. When the mixture starts to get hot, start stirring continuously.

5. The mixture will start to thicken as it gets hotter and reaches a slow boil. Let it quietly boil (keep stirring) for about 1 minute and then immediately remove it from the heat. If it starts to boil too strongly during the last minute of boiling, just lift the saucepan a little above the heat while continuing to stir.

6. Let the filling cool for about 5 minutes and then stir in the coconut.

7. Pour the filling into the waiting pie crust. Even the top out with a spatula if necessary.

8. After cooling, place the pie in refrigerator to chill thoroughly.

9. After the pie has been chilled, cover the filling with sweetened whipped cream and replace it in the refrigerator until ready to serve. If you wish, sprinkle a little plain or lightly toasted flaked coconut over the whipped cream.

Making the Sweetened Whipped Cream

1. Use heavy whipping cream instead of just plain whipping cream as it has a higher butterfat content and will make a firmer whipped cream.

2. Make sure that the bowl (preferably metal, and not too large) and the beaters, or whisk, that you will be using are cold. Put them in the freezer for a few minutes or in the refrigerator for 10 to 15 minutes before you start the process. Also make sure that the cream is well chilled.

3. Start mixing the cream at medium speed (in order to prevent splashing) and then at high speed after it has thickened a little.

4. When soft peaks are just starting to form, add the powdered sugar and vanilla and continue beating until the whipped cream is firm. Do not overbeat.

✦ Lemon Meringue Pie ✦

This recipe produces a great lemon meringue pie, complete with crispy crust, intense lemon filling and a white-as-a-cloud meringue topping. It looks too good to eat but most people can force themselves to do just that. This is one of America's favorite pies and it is equally at home in the see-through refrigerated shelf of a country diner as it is on a porcelain cake dish on your own dinner table. It is a dessert that truly deserves its popularity.

INGREDIENTS

1 prebaked 9-inch pie crust (see page 108)

For the Filling

$1^1/_2$ cups granulated sugar
7 tablespoons cornstarch
$^1/_4$ teaspoon salt
2 cups water
$^1/_2$ cup fresh squeezed lemon juice
4 large egg yolks
2 tablespoons salted butter
2 teaspoons grated lemon peel

For the Meringue

4 large egg whites
$^1/_4$ teaspoon cream of tartar
$^1/_2$ cup granulated sugar

Preheat the Oven

Set the oven to 350 degrees. Position the rack in the center of the oven.

Mixing the Filling

1. Put the sugar, cornstarch and salt into a medium-sized saucepan and whisk them together until no lumps of cornstarch remain.
2. Add the water and lemon juice and mix thoroughly.
3. Beat the egg yolks with a fork for 10 or 15 seconds, add them to the saucepan and mix thoroughly.
4. Turn the heat to medium and heat the mixture until it reaches a boil, stirring occasionally; stir continuously when it starts to get very hot.
5. Continue stirring until the mixture reaches a boil. Small bubbles will start to appear around the very edges, but do not consider this as reaching the boil. When the first larger bubbles appear, somewhere in the middle of the mixture, that is the boiling point. Boil for about 1 minute and then turn off the heat. The filling should be thick.
6. Stir in the butter until it melts. Add the lemon peel.
7. Immediately make the meringue, as you want to cover the pie with meringue while the filling is still hot.

Making the Meringue

Beat the egg whites at high speed until they are frothy. Add the cream of tartar and about a third of the sugar. Continue beating, add another third of the sugar in about a minute, and the remaining third a minute after that. Continue beating until the meringue holds a stiff peak when the whisk is lifted up. Do not overbeat; you want it stiff and shiny but not dry.

APPLYING THE MERINGUE

1. Pour the filling into the prebaked crust.
2. Using two spoons, one to scoop up and the other to push off the meringue, place the meringue evenly over the filling, making certain that the meringue always touches the edge of the crust. If you don't seal the meringue to the crust, it will shrink during baking.
3. Use your spoon to lift up small, swirling peaks in the meringue until your artistic sensibilities are satisfied.

BROWNING THE MERINGUE

1. Put the pie into the oven and bake until the meringue starts to brown. This should take about 10 minutes, but watch it carefully toward the end as you want the tips browned but not burned.
2. Remove the pie from the oven, let it cool down and then place it in the refrigerator for at least several hours before serving.

SERVING THE PIE

Because meringue is sticky and sometimes does not cut neatly, use a thin, sharp knife and, if at all possible, rinse it under hot water after each slice, or wipe down the knife with a clean, wet dish towel after each slice.

✦ Deep-Dish Apple Pie ✦

Perfected version of America's good old favorite, old-fashioned apple pie—this time *without* a bottom crust. This does make it easier to prepare and there is no bottom crust to get soggy with time, so you can keep it in the refrigerator for several days and then simply warm it up before serving. If you have a larger baking pan, you can increase the recipe and make enough to feed a crowd. A large attractive casserole of deep-dish apple pie, with a large spoon dug into it, alongside a bowl of ice cream or whipped cream, with a large spoon dug into that, makes a big hit on a buffet or picnic table.

Ingredients

Choose slightly tart cooking apples such as Granny Smith, Gravenstein, Baldwin, Pippin, Northern Spy, or even Golden Delicious, which is not particularly tart but holds its shape well in baking.

Pastry dough for 1 9-inch crust (see page 108)

For the Filling

- 10 medium-size apples (enough for 8 to 9 cups sliced), peeled, and cored and placed in a bowl of cold water
- 1 1/4 cups dark brown sugar, firmly packed (or 1 cup if apples are Golden Delicious)
- 4 tablespoons all-purpose flour
- 1 1/2 teaspoons cinnamon
- 1 teaspoon lemon juice (or 2 teaspoons if apples are Golden Delicious)
- 2 tablespoons salted butter

For the Glaze

1 large egg
¼ cup milk
1 to 2 tablespoons granulated sugar

PREPARE YOUR BAKING PAN

Do not grease or butter the inside of the baking pan. Use a 13 × 9 × 2-inch glass, porcelain or metal baking pan. A glass or porcelain baking dish will make the best presentation at the table. Whichever baking dish you will be using you will want the apples to be at least 1½ to 1¾ inches deep.

PREHEAT THE OVEN

Set the oven to 400 degrees. Place the rack in the center of the oven and place a cookie sheet on the rack to catch any drippings.

PREPARING THE FILLING

1. Put the sugar, flour, cinnamon and lemon juice into a large bowl and mix them together.
2. Slice the apples fairly thin, add them to the brown sugar mixture and toss until they are coated evenly.
3. Place the apples into the baking pan.
4. Cut the cold butter into bits and scatter it evenly over the apples. Set aside.

PREPARE THE CRUST

1. Using the recipe for single-crust pastry dough (see page 101), roll out the dough in a shape large enough to cover the top of the baking dish.
2. Lay the dough over the dish, trim off any excess and push the edges down around the sides. You don't have to seal the crust to the dish but if you would like to, you certainly can.
3. Brush the top crust with a mixture of the egg and milk but don't leave puddles on the dough. Sprinkle a small amount of sugar evenly across the top.
4. Cut three or four vents in the crust to release the steam while baking. Make several small circles or triangles or $1/8$-inch-wide slits. Then place the pie in the oven.

BAKING THE PIE

Bake for 50 to 60 minutes until the filling is bubbling hot, the crust is nicely browned and the apples are tender when pierced with a fork or knife. It is better to overbake a little than underbake. If the crust starts to get too brown, just cover the pie with a large piece of aluminum foil.

COOLING THE PIE

Let the pie cool on a wire rack. As the pie cools, some of the liquid will be reabsorbed.

SERVING THE PIE

Serve slightly warm or at room temperature. It can be served with an accompanying scoop of vanilla ice cream or with a dollop of whipped cream or just by itself.

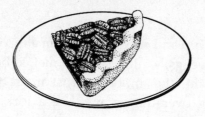

✦ Pecan Pie ✦

Pecan pie is one of the South's great contributions to America's desserts and almost everyone loves it. It's rich and delicious and calorie counters will just have to consider this an exception to their diet. It is an irresistible treat.

INGREDIENTS

1 prebaked 9-inch pie crust (see page 108)

For the Filling

½ cup light corn syrup
1 cup dark brown sugar, firmly packed
3 large eggs, beaten
2 teaspoons vanilla
½ teaspoon salt
4 tablespoons (½ stick) salted butter, melted
1 cup pecan halves or pieces

PREHEAT THE OVEN

Set the oven to 350 degrees. Position the rack in the center of the oven.

MIXING THE FILLING

1. Stir the corn syrup and sugar together in a mixing bowl.
2. Add the beaten eggs, vanilla, salt and melted butter and blend well.
3. Put the pecans into the empty pie crust and settle them down evenly.
4. Pour the filling over the pecans. Use a fork, if necessary, to push the pecans down evenly across the surface.

BAKING THE PIE

Bake for 30 to 35 minutes until the pie looks set all over and even the very center doesn't shimmy when you gently move the pie in the oven. Keep a close watch at the end of the baking cycle as you don't want to overbake the pie.

COOLING THE PIE

Cool the pie completely on a wire rack. Let it reach room temperature before you serve it. Or if you want to serve it much later or the next day, store it in the refrigerator and then let it reach room temperature before serving it. You can, if you like, also serve it slightly warm, and if you sneak a leftover piece right from the refrigerator on the following day, you'll also love it.

NOTE

Because the crust is already prebaked and the edges lightly browned, you can cover the pie with a tent of aluminum foil if it looks like it might be over-browning while baking. Tent the aluminum foil over the pie so the foil doesn't touch the filling.

✦ Pumpkin Pie ✦

Pumpkin pie goes back to early Colonial days and for good reason—it's wonderful, and it is such a mistake to relegate it to a once-a-year serving on Thanksgiving day. Rich, smooth and creamy, delicately spiced with cinnamon and ginger and cloves and nutmeg and allspice, it is a treasure house of flavor. When made outside of the Thanksgiving holiday, it invariably gets, first, a look of surprise, and then, a smile of anticipation. In other words, keep this recipe handy.

INGREDIENTS

1 prebaked 9-inch pie crust (see page 108)

For the Filling

2 cups (one 16-ounce can) pumpkin puree (solid-pack pumpkin, not pumpkin-pie mix)
3/4 cup dark brown sugar, firmly packed
1 1/2 cups half-and-half (or 1 cup milk plus 1/2 cup whipping cream, or one 12-ounce can of evaporated milk)
1/2 teaspoon salt
1 teaspoon cinnamon
1/2 teaspoon ginger
1/4 teaspoon ground cloves
1/4 teaspoon nutmeg
1/4 teaspoon allspice
2 large eggs
2 large egg yolks

PREHEAT THE OVEN

Set the oven to 350 degrees. Position the rack in the center of the oven. Place a cookie sheet on the rack.

PREPARING THE FILLING

1. Thoroughly stir the pumpkin and sugar together in a large mixing bowl.
2. Add 1¼ cups of the half-and-half or milk and cream and stir the mixture together. To the remaining ¼ cup, add the salt and all the spices. Stir everything together and add it to the large bowl.
3. Beat the eggs and yolks together for a few seconds and add this to the mixture.
4. Using a large whisk or a heavy spoon, stir the mixture until it is smooth and uniform in appearance.
5. Pour the filling into the prebaked pie crust. Don't fill it so close to the top of the crust that it spills over the top when you move it. You can fill it three-quarters full and pour some more filling in after you have placed it in the oven and don't have to move it again.

BAKING THE PIE

Bake the pie anywhere from 45 to 60 minutes (depending on the oven) until the pie looks set except possibly for the very center (about 1 inch in diameter), which could shimmy ever so slightly when you move the pan. You should take it out then, as the very center will set up after the pie is removed from the oven. If the very center is already set and doesn't quiver at the time you check it, that's all right. Just remove it at once. Keep a close watch at the end of the baking cycle as you don't want to overbake the pie.

COOLING THE PIE

Cool the pie completely on a wire rack. Or if you want to serve it much later or the next day, store it in the refrigerator.

SERVING THE PIE

Serve slightly warmed or at room temperature. You can serve it with a bowl of lightly sweetened whipped cream. Refrigerate any left over.

NOTE

Because the crust is already prebaked and the edges lightly browned, you can cover the pie with a tent of aluminum foil if it looks like it might be overbrowning while baking. To make the tent, fold a large enough piece of aluminum foil in half and place it over the pie. Make sure the foil doesn't touch the pumpkin filling.

✦ Apple Cobbler ✦

Apple cobblers are a part of that conglomeration of old-fashioned fruit desserts with exotic names like crisp, buckle, grunt, pandowdy and slump. They are all very, very good but the test of time has put the apple cobbler at or near the top of the list. If you love apple pie (and who doesn't) you'll love apple cobbler, with its sweet biscuit topping.

INGREDIENTS

For the Apple Filling

Use tart cooking apples such as Granny Smith, Pippin, Gravenstein, Baldwin, Northern Spy or Golden Delicious, an eating rather than a cooking apple and less tart, but still very good to use because it holds its shape and is widely available. You will need enough apples to fill almost to the top the size dish you are using (see below).

3/4 cup dark brown sugar, firmly packed (or 1/2 cup if apples are
   Golden Delicious)
2 tablespoons cornstarch
1 teaspoon cinnamon
1/4 teaspoon nutmeg
8 to 9 apples, cored, peeled, cut into quarters and sliced thin (about
   7 cups)
1 teaspoon lemon juice
2 tablespoons salted butter

For the Topping

1   cup all-purpose flour
1½   teaspoons baking powder
¼   teaspoon salt
3   tablespoons granulated sugar
2   ounces (½ stick) salted butter, at room temperature
½   teaspoon vanilla
½   cup milk

Premeasure and lay out all your ingredients on the counter.

PREPARE YOUR BAKING PAN

Do not grease or butter the inside of the baking pan. For the amount of filling in this recipe use an 8 × 8 × 2-inch or a 9 × 9 × 2-inch square baking pan or glass baking dish or the equivalent in a round casserole. A glass or porcelain baking dish will make the best presentation at the table. You will want the apples to be at least 1½ to 1¾ inches deep.

PREHEAT THE OVEN

Set the oven to 375 degrees. Position the rack in the center of the oven. You could also put a small sheet of aluminum foil on a rack underneath to catch any possible spills.

PREPARING THE FILLING

1.   In a large bowl, mix together the dark brown sugar, cornstarch, cinnamon and nutmeg and blend them together thoroughly.

2. Add the apples and the lemon juice and stir everything together.
3. Using a spatula, push the filling and all the liquid into the baking pan or dish and even out the top.
4. Cut the butter into bits and scatter it over the top.
5. Put the cobbler in the oven *without the topping* and cover it loosely with a piece of aluminum foil.
6. Bake the cobbler (with the aluminum foil on top) for 30 minutes to soften up the apples. If you are using Golden Delicious apples, bake for only 15 minutes.

PREPARING THE TOPPING

(You can do this after the cobbler goes into the oven.)

1. Put the flour, baking powder, salt and granulated sugar into a mixing bowl and stir them together.
2. Cut the butter into several pieces and add to the flour mixture.
3. Using a pastry blender or two knives or your fingers, cut the butter into the flour so that the mixture is like a very coarse meal, with little bits of butter showing.
   Note: If you prefer to use a food processor, use cold butter and, when finished, turn out the mixture into a bowl.
4. Add the vanilla and the milk and stir everything together until you have a soft and somewhat sticky dough that will hold its shape when picked up with a spoon.

FINISHING THE COBBLER

1. Remove the cobbler from the oven and, using a large spoon, drop the top-

ping over the filling evenly in about nine places in a checkerboard pattern, letting the filling show between each as well as you can. If a couple of them run together, that's all right. It will just add to the handmade appearance. The dough will be sticky so you can use a wet finger to push it off the large spoon exactly where you want it.

2. Sprinkle a little granulated sugar over each mound of batter.
3. Put the cobbler back into the oven to finish baking, this time without the aluminum foil.

Baking the Cobbler

Bake the cobbler until the apples are tender and the topping is browned. This should take about another 30 minutes, depending on the type of apples used. If the topping seems brown enough but the apples are not quite tender, just cover the cobbler with a piece of aluminum foil for the remainder of the baking period.

Cooling and Serving the Cobbler

If the filling is a bit runny it will firm up as it cools. Although it is delicious at room temperature, it is at its very best when served warm with a large scoop of vanilla ice cream.

✦ Peach Cobbler ✦

Peach cobblers always evoke a delicious memory of summertime, but a piece of warm peach cobbler served with whipped cream or vanilla ice cream is a special dessert for any meal. There is something especially delightful in having a luscious fruit dessert when that fruit is ripe and in season. If you like, you can make this same cobbler using other ripe fruit such as apricots or nectarines.

For the Peach Filling

- 3/4 cup granulated sugar
- 3 tablespoons cornstarch
- 1/4 teaspoon cinnamon
- 1/4 teaspoon nutmeg
- 6 cups sliced fresh peaches
- 1 tablespoon lemon juice

For the Topping

- 1 cup all-purpose flour
- 1 1/2 teaspoons baking powder
- 1/4 teaspoon salt
- 3 tablespoons granulated sugar
- 2 ounces (1/2 stick) salted butter, at room temperature
- 1/2 teaspoon vanilla
- 1/2 cup milk

Premeasure and lay out all your ingredients on the counter.

PREPARE YOUR BAKING PAN

For the amount of filling in this recipe use an 8 × 8 × 2-inch baking pan or glass baking dish, or its equivalent in a small round casserole. A glass or porcelain casserole or baking dish will make the best presentation at the table. You do not have to grease or butter the inside of the baking pan or dish. The peaches should be at least 1½ to 1¾ inches deep. If you use a larger baking dish for a larger number of diners or for a party, just increase the ingredients proportionately.

PREHEAT THE OVEN

Set the oven to 375 degrees. Position the rack in the center of the oven.

PREPARING THE FILLING

1. In a large bowl mix together the sugar, cornstarch, cinnamon and nutmeg and blend them together thoroughly.
2. Add the peaches and lemon juice and stir everything together carefully.
3. Pour the fruit mixture into the baking pan or dish and press down to even out the top.

PREPARING THE TOPPING

1. Combine the flour, baking powder, salt and sugar in a mixing bowl.
2. Cut the butter into several smaller pieces and drop the pieces into the bowl.
3. Using a pastry blender, two knives or your fingers, cut the butter into the flour until the texture is like a very coarse meal, with little bits of butter remaining.

   Note: If you prefer to use a food processor, use cold butter and, when finished, turn out the mixture into a bowl.

4. Add the vanilla and the milk and mix everything together until you have a soft and somewhat sticky dough that will hold its shape when picked up with a spoon.

FINISHING THE COBBLER

1. Drop about 9 rounded tablespoons of topping over the filling in a checkerboard pattern, letting a little filling show between each spoonful. It's all right if some of them run together while baking. The dough will be sticky so use a wet finger to push it off the spoon exactly where you want it.
2. Sprinkle a little granulated sugar over each mound of batter.

BAKING THE COBBLER

Bake the cobbler until the peaches are soft when pierced with the tip of a sharp knife and the topping is browned. This should take 45 to 60 minutes.

COOLING AND SERVING

Let the cobbler cool because it will firm up as it cools. Although it's delicious at room temperature, it's at its very best when served warm and juicy with a scoop of vanilla ice cream.

✦ Apple Crisp ✦

This is so easy to make and so delicious to eat that every time I have it I wonder why I let so much time elapse since the last one. The aroma of tart, fresh apples being heated with butter and spices is, in itself, intoxicating. Add to that the aroma of the crisp topping being baked on top of the bubbling apples and you know you are in for a treat—and you are. It is great with or without vanilla ice cream, as long as it is served slightly warm.

For the Topping

- 1 cup all-purpose flour
- ¹/₂ cup dark brown sugar, firmly packed
- ³/₄ teaspoon cinnamon
- ¹/₈ teaspoon salt
- 3 ounces (³/₄ stick) salted butter, at room temperature

For the Apple Filling

Use tart cooking apples such as Granny Smith, Pippin, Gravenstein, Baldwin, Northern Spy or Golden Delicious, an eating rather than a cooking apple and less tart, but still very good to use because it holds its shape and is widely available.

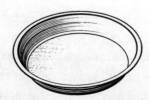

$3/4$ cup dark brown sugar, firmly packed (or only $1/2$ cup sugar if using
    Golden Delicious apples)
$1^1/2$ tablespoons cornstarch
  1 teaspoon cinnamon
$1/4$ teaspoon nutmeg
  1 teaspoon lemon juice (or $1^1/2$ teaspoons if apples are Golden Delicious)
  8 to 9 apples, cored, peeled, cut into quarters and sliced thin (about
    7 cups)
  2 tablespoons salted butter

Premeasure and lay out all your ingredients on the counter.

PREPARE YOUR BAKING PAN

Do not grease or butter the inside of the baking pan. For the amount of
filling in this recipe use an 8 × 8 × 2-inch or a 9 × 9 × 2-inch baking pan or
glass baking dish or the equivalent in a round casserole. A glass or porcelain
baking dish will make the best presentation at the table. You will want the
apples to be at least $1^1/2$ to $1^3/4$ inches deep.

PREHEAT THE OVEN

Set the oven to 375 degrees. Position the rack in the center of the oven. You can
also put a small sheet of aluminum foil on a rack underneath to catch any spills.

PREPARING THE TOPPING

1. Put the flour, sugar, cinnamon and salt into a mixing bowl and stir them
   together until no lumps of brown sugar remain.
2. Cut the butter into several pieces and drop the pieces into the bowl.
3. Using a pastry blender or two knives or your fingers, cut the butter into the flour
   so that the mixture is like a very coarse meal, with little bits of butter showing.

4. Using your fingertips, squeeze the mixture together so that it looks lumpy, like coarse crumbs. Put it aside for later use.

   Note: If you prefer using the food processor for steps 1, 2, and 3, use cold butter and then transfer the resulting coarse mixture to a bowl and use your fingertips as described in Step 4.

PREPARING THE FILLING

1. In a large bowl mix the sugar, cornstarch, cinnamon and nutmeg. Blend them together thoroughly.
2. Add the apples and the lemon juice and stir everything together carefully.
3. Using a spatula, push the filling and all the liquid into the baking pan or dish and even out the top.
4. Cut the butter into bits and scatter it over the filling.
5. Put the crisp in the oven *without the topping* and cover it loosely with a piece of aluminum foil.

BAKING THE CRISP

1. Bake the crisp (with the piece of aluminum foil on top) for 30 minutes to soften up the apples a bit. If you are using Golden Delicious apples, bake for only 15 minutes.
2. Remove the crisp from the oven and gently stir the apples and juice together. Then spoon the topping evenly over the filling, and put the crisp back into the oven to finish baking, this time without the aluminum foil.
3. Bake until the apples are tender and the topping is well browned. This should take about another 30 minutes, depending on the type of apples used.

COOLING AND SERVING THE CRISP

If the filling is a bit runny, it will firm up as it cools. Although it's delicious at room temperature, it's at its very best when served warm with a large scoop of vanilla ice cream.

✦ Blueberry Crisp ✦

Celebrate the blueberry season with a fragrant, juicy and super-delicious blueberry crisp. Although fresh blueberries are ideal when they are in season, as are wild blueberries if you are lucky enough to have them available, do not ignore the unsweetened, frozen ones that are available year round in the freezer section of your local market. If you didn't know ahead of time, you probably couldn't tell the difference. Incidentally, you can use other berries such as blackberries, boysenberries, olallieberries and the like, and follow this same recipe to arrive at the berry crisp of your dreams.

For the Blueberry Filling

- 1/4 cup cold water
- 3 tablespoons cornstarch
- 2/3 cup granulated sugar
- 6 cups blueberries, fresh or unsweetened frozen
- 1 tablespoon lemon juice

For the Topping

- 1 cup all-purpose flour
- 1/2 cup dark brown sugar, firmly packed
- 3/4 teaspoon cinnamon
- 1/8 teaspoon salt
- 3 ounces (3/4 stick) salted butter, at room temperature

Premeasure and lay out all your ingredients on the counter.

Prepare Your Baking Pan

For the amount of filling in this recipe use an 8 × 8 × 2-inch metal or glass baking dish or its equivalent in a small round casserole. A glass or porcelain casserole or baking dish will make the best presentation at the table. Do not grease or butter the baking dish. You will want the blueberries to be at least 1½ to 1¾ inches deep. If you want a larger crisp, just increase the ingredients proportionately.

Preheat the Oven

Set the oven to 375 degrees. Position the rack in the center of the oven.

Preparing the Filling

1. In a large bowl mix together the water and cornstarch. Then stir in the sugar.
2. Add the blueberries and lemon juice and combine thoroughly.
3. Pour the fruit mixture into the baking dish and even out the top.

Preparing the Topping

1. Put the flour, brown sugar, cinnamon and salt into a large mixing bowl and stir them together until there are no lumps of brown sugar.
2. Cut the butter into several pieces and drop the pieces into the bowl.
3. Using a pastry blender, two knives, or your fingers, work the butter into the flour until the texture is like a very coarse meal.

Finishing the Crisp

Spread the topping evenly over the blueberries and gently press down with a spatula or your fingers (I use my fingers) so that the topping completely covers the fruit.

Baking the Crisp

Bake the crisp for 40 to 45 minutes, or until the topping is well browned.

Cooling and Serving the Crisp

Let the crisp cool because it will firm up a bit. Although it's delicious at room temperature, it's at its very best when served warm and juicy with a scoop of vanilla ice cream.

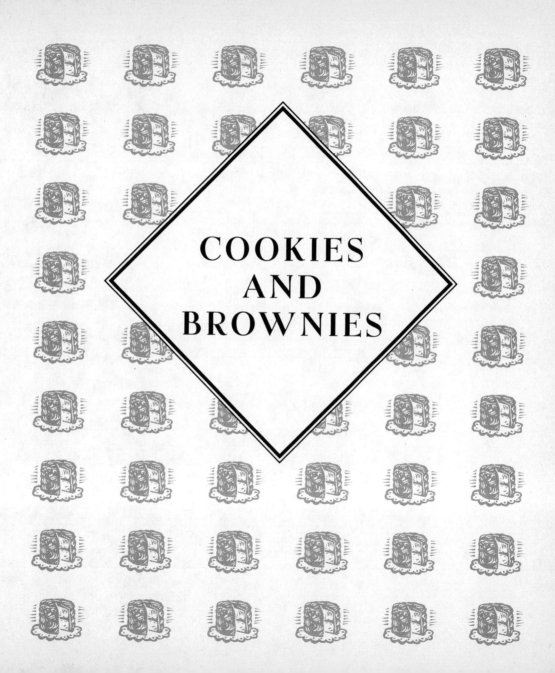

COOKIES
AND
BROWNIES

✦ Chocolate Chip Cookies ✦

The Toll House Inn in Massachusetts is where this cookie was conceived in the 1930s and there is no place in America now where it is not the Number One cookie in popularity. This recipe makes a super-delicious chocolate chip cookie.

INGREDIENTS

8	ounces (2 sticks) salted butter, at room temperature
3/4	cup dark brown sugar, firmly packed
3/4	cup granulated sugar
1 1/2	teaspoons vanilla
2	large eggs
2	cups all-purpose flour
1/2	teaspoon baking soda
1/2	teaspoon salt
2	cups (one 12-ounce bag) chocolate chips, semisweet
1	cup walnuts, in small pieces

Premeasure and lay out all your ingredients on the counter.

PREPARE YOUR BAKING PAN

Grease a cookie sheet lightly and evenly with solid shortening or cover it with a piece of baking parchment paper cut to fit.

PREHEAT THE OVEN

Set the oven to 375 degrees. Position the rack in the upper third of the oven. If you want to bake two trays of cookies at the same time, use the top and middle shelves of the oven and, midway through the baking, switch the trays and rotate them front to back at the same time.

MIXING THE DOUGH

1. In a bowl, using a mixer, cream the butter, both sugars and the vanilla at high speed for several minutes until the mixture is smooth and light.
2. Add the eggs and mix them in.
3. Thoroughly blend together the flour, baking soda and salt, add them to the mixing bowl and beat until they are just blended in. Do not overbeat.
4. At low speed, or by hand with a large rubber spatula, blend in the chocolate chips and the walnuts.
5. Deposit the cookies on the cookie sheet by rounded tablespoonfuls in even rows, with space between to allow for spreading. You can use a second spoon, or even your finger, to push the dough off the first spoon onto the cookie sheet. Have a glass of water handy in which to dip your spoons occasionally; this will make the depositing easier and faster. Round off each cookie neatly and push together any ragged edges carefully.

BAKING THE COOKIES

Bake for 12 to 18 minutes or until the tops of the cookies look set and are starting to turn brown.

COOLING THE COOKIES

Let the cookies cool on the cookie sheet for a minute or two until they can be transferred easily to cooling racks. They can also be placed on sheets of wax paper to finish cooling if you don't have enough racks. If you are using baking parchment paper, you can just slide the entire sheet of cookies onto a suitable counter and leave them there until completely cooled, while you use the cookie sheet for the next batch of cookies.

✦ Chocolate Cookies ✦

MAKES 22 2¹/₂-INCH COOKIES

A cookie collection without a pure and basic chocolate cookie would be unthinkable, and so here is one I particularly like. Easy to make, it should satisfy the craving for something chocolate that mysteriously arises in everyone from time to time.

INGREDIENTS

3	ounces (³/₄ stick) salted butter, at room temperature
1	cup granulated sugar
1	large egg
1	cup all-purpose flour
¹/₃	cup cocoa, unsweetened
¹/₄	teaspoon baking soda
¹/₄	teaspoon salt
¹/₄	cup water
1	teaspoon vanilla
¹/₂	cup walnuts, finely chopped

Premeasure and lay out all your ingredients on the counter.

PREPARE YOUR BAKING PAN

Grease a cookie sheet lightly and evenly with solid shortening or cover it with a piece of baking parchment paper cut to fit.

PREHEAT THE OVEN

Set the oven to 350 degrees. Position the rack in the upper third of the oven. If you want to bake two trays of cookies at the same time, use the top and middle shelves of the oven and, midway through the baking, switch the trays and rotate them front to back at the same time.

MIXING THE DOUGH

1. In a bowl, using a mixer, cream the butter and sugar at high speed for several minutes until the mixture is smooth and light.
2. Add the egg and mix it in.
3. Thoroughly blend together the flour, cocoa, baking soda and salt, add them to the mixing bowl and beat until they are just blended in. Do not overbeat.
4. Add and blend in the water and the vanilla.
5. At low speed, blend in the walnuts.
6. Deposit the cookies on the cookie sheet by rounded teaspoonfuls in even rows, with space between to allow for some spreading. You can use a second spoon, or even your wet finger, to push the dough off the first spoon onto the cookie sheet. Have a glass of water handy in which to dip your spoons occasionally; this will make the depositing easier and faster. After depositing the cookie dough on the cookie sheet, round it off and push in any ragged edges with your fingers. Before putting the cookie sheet in the oven, gently push down the top of each cookie with your wet fingers as neatly and evenly as possible. Just a little flattening will do, but try to make them all the same thickness for even baking.

BAKING THE COOKIES

Bake for 14 to 20 minutes or until the tops of the cookies look set and are just starting to turn brown. You can use a spatula to gently lift the edge of a cookie to see if it looks done on the bottom.

COOLING THE COOKIES

Let the cookies cool on the cookie sheet for a minute or two until they can be transferred easily to racks. They can also be placed on sheets of wax paper to finish cooling if you don't have enough racks. If you are using baking parchment paper, you can just slide the entire sheet of cookies onto a suitable counter and leave them there until completely cooled, while you use the cookie sheet for the next batch of cookies.

◆ Coconut Macaroons ◆

MAKES APPROXIMATELY 20 MACAROONS

With just a few ingredients to mix, this is a dream cookie for coconut lovers. Sweet, coconutty and chewy, they are an easy and great addition to the cookie scene.

INGREDIENTS

- 2 large egg whites
- 1/4 teaspoon cream of tartar
- 1/3 cup granulated sugar
- 2 tablespoons all-purpose flour
- 1/8 teaspoon salt
- 1 teaspoon vanilla
- 2 cups sweetened flaked coconut (You can also use shredded coconut if you wish.)

Premeasure and lay out all your ingredients on the counter.

PREPARE YOUR BAKING PAN

Grease a cookie sheet evenly with solid shortening or cover it with a piece of baking parchment paper cut to fit.

PREHEAT THE OVEN

Set the oven to 325 degrees. Position the rack in the upper third of the oven. If you want to bake two trays of macaroons at the same time, use the top and middle shelves of the oven and, midway through the baking, switch the trays and rotate them front to back at the same time.

MIXING THE BATTER

1. In a clean, dry bowl, beat the egg whites until they are frothy. Add the cream of tartar and then continue beating until soft, wet peaks are formed, adding the sugar gradually as you beat. Beat until the peaks stand up straight when you lift the beaters. Do not overbeat. The peaks should be shiny when you are finished and overbeating will make them dry.
2. Gently mix in the flour, salt, vanilla and coconut.
3. Drop the batter by rounded teaspoonfuls on the prepared cookie sheet. Shape as neatly as possible with your fingers.

BAKING THE MACAROONS

Bake until the macaroons are lightly browned, 18 to 22 minutes.

COOLING THE MACAROONS

Let the macaroons cool on the cookie sheet for a minute or two until they can be transferred easily to racks. They can also be placed on sheets of wax paper to finish cooling if you don't have enough racks. If you are using baking parchment paper, you can just slide the entire sheet of cookies onto a suitable counter and leave them there until completely cooled, while you use the cookie sheet for the next batch.

NOTE

Some bakers fold the 2 egg yolks (well beaten) into the batter before placing it on the cookie sheet; this makes an interesting variation. Done this way, it will take a few minutes longer to bake.

✦ Ginger Cookies ✦

MAKES 30 2¹/₂-INCH COOKIES

Ginger, molasses and cinnamon combine to produce a haunting, spicy flavor that lingers on and on. Don't worry about the largish amount of ground ginger that goes into the recipe—it needs it.

Ingredients

2	cups all-purpose flour
2	teaspoons baking soda
3	teaspoons ground ginger
¹/₂	teaspoon cinnamon
¹/₄	teaspoon ground cloves
¹/₂	teaspoon salt
1	cup granulated sugar
1	large egg
¹/₂	cup vegetable oil (canola or safflower)
¹/₄	cup molasses (light preferred)
2	tablespoons water

Premeasure and lay out all your ingredients on the counter.

Prepare Your Baking Pan

Grease a cookie sheet lightly and evenly with solid shortening or cover it with a piece of baking parchment paper cut to fit.

Preheat the Oven

Set the oven to 350 degrees. Position the rack in the upper third of the oven. If you want to bake two trays of cookies at the same time, use the top and middle shelves of the oven and, midway through the baking, switch the trays and rotate them front to back at the same time.

Mixing the Dough

1. In a bowl, combine the flour, baking soda, ginger, cinnamon, cloves and salt.
2. In a second bowl, using a mixer, combine the sugar, egg, oil, molasses and water. Add the flour-spice mixture and mix until the batter is well blended together.
3. Deposit the dough on the cookie sheet by rounded teaspoonfuls in even rows, with space between to allow for some spreading. You can use a second spoon, or even your finger, to push the dough off the first spoon onto the cookie sheet. Have a glass of water handy in which to dip your spoons occasionally; this will make the depositing easier and faster. After depositing the cookie dough on the cookie sheet you can round it off and push in any ragged edges with your fingers. Before putting the cookie sheet in the oven, gently push down the top of each cookie with your wet fingers. Just a little flattening will do, but try to make them all the same thickness for even baking.

Baking the Cookies

Bake for 16 to 20 minutes or until the tops of the cookies look set and are starting to turn brown. You can use a spatula to gently lift the edge of a cookie to see if it looks done on the bottom.

COOLING THE COOKIES

Let the cookies cool on the cookie sheet for a minute or two until they can be transferred easily to racks. They can also be placed on sheets of wax paper to finish cooling if you don't have enough racks. If you are using baking parchment paper, you can just slide the entire sheet of cookies onto a suitable counter and you can leave them there until completely cooled, while you use the cookie sheet for the next batch of cookies.

✦ Hermits ✦

MAKES 24 2¹/₂-INCH COOKIES

This is part of a collection of old-time New England cookies with funny names like Snickerdoodles, Jolly Boys and Kinkawoodles. Hermits have out-lasted most of the others in popularity and for good reason. Made with dark brown sugar, molasses, lots of spices and plenty of raisins and walnuts, they make a lasting impression.

INGREDIENTS

- 1¹/₂ cups all-purpose flour
- 2 teaspoons baking powder
- ¹/₄ teaspoon salt
- 1¹/₂ teaspoons cinnamon
- ¹/₄ teaspoon nutmeg
- ¹/₄ teaspoon ground cloves
- ¹/₄ teaspoon allspice
- 4 ounces (1 stick) salted butter, at room temperature
- ³/₄ cup dark brown sugar, firmly packed
- 1 large egg
- 2 tablespoons molasses (light or dark)
- 1 teaspoon vanilla
- ¹/₄ cup milk
- 1 cup walnuts, finely chopped
- 1 cup raisins (rinsed briefly in hot water)

Premeasure and lay out all your ingredients on the counter. Lightly com-bine the flour, baking powder, salt and spices.

Prepare Your Baking Pan

Grease a cookie sheet lightly and evenly with solid shortening or cover it with a piece of baking parchment paper cut to fit.

Preheat the Oven

Set the oven to 375 degrees. Position the rack in the upper third of the oven. If you want to bake two trays of cookies at the same time, use the top and middle shelves of the oven and, midway through the baking, switch the trays and rotate them front to back at the same time.

Mixing the Dough

1. In a large bowl, using a mixer, beat the butter at high speed until it is soft and smooth, about 1 minute.
2. Add the sugar and continue beating at medium speed until the mixture is light and fluffy.
3. Mixing at medium speed, add the egg, molasses and vanilla, beating only until they are well blended. Remember to scrape down the bowl.
4. Add half of the combined dry ingredients and half of the milk and mix at medium speed for about 20 seconds. Do this one more time and then beat

the dough for about 1 minute or so, until it is uniform and smooth looking. Do not overbeat.

5. At low speed, or by hand with a large rubber spatula, blend in the walnuts and the raisins.

6. Deposit the dough on the cookie sheet by heaping teaspoonfuls in even rows, with space between to allow for spreading. You can use a second spoon, or even your finger, to push the dough off the first spoon onto the cookie sheet. Have a glass of water handy in which to dip your spoons occasionally; this will make the depositing easier and faster. With the fingers of both hands, round off each cookie neatly and push together any ragged edges carefully. Do not flatten them down more than is necessary to keep them fairly uniform in height.

BAKING THE COOKIES

Bake for 14 to 20 minutes (it depends on the size of the cookies) until the tops of the cookies look set and are starting to turn brown.

COOLING THE COOKIES

Let the cookies cool on the cookie sheet for a minute or two until they can be transferred easily to racks. They can also be placed on sheets of wax paper to finish cooling if you don't have enough racks. If you are using baking parchment paper, you can just slide the entire sheet of cookies onto a suitable counter and leave them there until completely cooled, while you use the cookie sheet for the next batch of cookies.

✦ Oatmeal-Raisin Cookies ✦

MAKES 22 2½- INCH COOKIES

A little crunchy and a little chewy best describes my version of this great American cookie. I use old-fashioned oats rather than quick oats because it adds to both the texture and the flavor.

INGREDIENTS

4	ounces (1 stick) salted butter, at room temperature
¾	cup dark brown sugar, firmly packed
½	teaspoon vanilla
1	large egg
¾	cup all-purpose flour
½	teaspoon baking soda
½	teaspoon cinnamon
⅛	teaspoon nutmeg
¼	teaspoon salt
1½	cups rolled oats (old-fashioned, not quick-cooking)
½	cup raisins (rinsed briefly in hot water)

Premeasure and lay out all your ingredients on the counter.

PREPARE YOUR BAKING PAN

Grease a cookie sheet lightly and evenly with solid shortening or cover it with a piece of baking parchment paper cut to fit.

PREHEAT THE OVEN

Set the oven to 350 degrees. Position the rack in the upper third of the oven. If you want to bake two trays of cookies at the same time, use the top and middle shelves of the oven and, midway through the baking, switch the trays and rotate them front to back at the same time.

MIXING THE DOUGH

1. In a bowl, using a mixer, cream the butter, sugar and the vanilla at high speed for several minutes until the mixture is smooth and light.
2. Add the egg and mix it in.
3. Thoroughly blend together the flour, baking soda, cinnamon, nutmeg and salt, add them to the mixing bowl and beat until they are just blended. Do not overbeat.
4. Add and blend in the rolled oats and then the raisins.
5. Deposit the dough on the cookie sheet by rounded teaspoonfuls in even rows, with space between to allow for some spreading. You can use a second spoon, or even your finger, to push the dough off the first spoon onto the cookie sheet. Have a glass of water handy in which to dip your spoons occasionally; this will make the depositing easier and faster.

     You now have a choice. You can pick up each cookie and very gently roll it between the palms of your hands to make a rounded ball which you will then put back on the cookie sheet. Or, if you prefer, after depositing the cookie dough on the cookie sheet you could round it off and push in any ragged edges with your fingers.

     Before putting the cookie sheet in the oven, gently push down the top of each cookie with your wet fingers. Just a little flattening will do, but try to make them all the same thickness for even baking.

BAKING THE COOKIES

Bake for 12 to 15 minutes or until the tops of the cookies look set and are just starting to turn brown. You can use a spatula to gently lift the edge of a cookie to see if it looks done on the bottom.

COOLING THE COOKIES

Let the cookies cool on the cookie sheet for a minute or two until they can be transferred easily to racks. They can also be placed on sheets of wax paper to finish cooling if you don't have enough racks. If you are using baking parchment paper, you can just slide the entire sheet of cookies onto a suitable counter and leave them there until completely cooled, while you use the cookie sheet for the next batch of cookies.

✦ Peanut Butter Cookies ✦

MAKES 40 2-INCH COOKIES

Another national favorite. I prefer the kind made with chunky peanut butter, as in this recipe, but happily eat those made with the smooth and creamy kind. Either way, these must be in your cookie collection. Kids love them.

INGREDIENTS

- 4 ounces (1 stick) salted butter, at room temperature
- 6 tablespoons granulated sugar
- 6 tablespoons dark brown sugar, firmly packed
- 1 teaspoon vanilla
- 1 large egg
- 2/3 cup chunky peanut butter (if available, use the natural kind without added sweetening)
- 1 cup all-purpose flour
- 1/4 teaspoon baking soda
- 1/4 teaspoon salt

Premeasure and lay out all your ingredients on the counter.

Prepare Your Baking Pan

Grease a cookie sheet lightly and evenly with solid shortening or cover it with a piece of baking parchment paper cut to fit.

Preheat the Oven

Set the oven to 375 degrees. Position the rack in the upper third of the oven. If you want to bake two trays of cookies at the same time, use the top and middle shelves of the oven and, midway through the baking, switch the trays and rotate them front to back at the same time.

Mixing the Dough

1. In a bowl, using a mixer, cream the butter, both sugars and the vanilla at high speed for several minutes until the mixture is smooth and light.
2. Mix in the egg.
3. Add the peanut butter and mix it in. Scrape the bowl down once or twice.
4. Thoroughly blend together the flour, baking soda and salt, add them to the mixing bowl and beat until they are just blended. Do not overbeat.
5. Deposit the cookies on the cookie sheet by rounded teaspoonfuls in even rows, with space between to allow for some spreading. You can use a second spoon, or even your finger, to push the dough off the first spoon onto the cookie sheet. Have a glass of water handy in which to dip your spoons occasionally; this will make the depositing easier and faster.

You now have a choice. You can pick up each cookie and very gently roll it between the palms of your hands to make a rounded ball which you will then put back on the cookie sheet. Or, if you prefer, after depositing the cookie dough on the cookie sheet you could round it off and push in any ragged edges with your wet fingers.

Before putting the cookie sheet in the oven, gently press down the top of each cookie with the tines of a wet fork to make the traditional crisscross design usually associated with peanut butter cookies.

BAKING THE COOKIES

Bake for about 15 minutes, until the tops of the cookies look set and are starting to turn brown. You can use a spatula to gently lift the edge of a cookie to see if it looks brown on the bottom.

COOLING THE COOKIES

Let the cookies cool on the cookie sheet for a minute or two until they are cooled enough to be transferred easily to racks. They can also be placed on sheets of wax paper to finish cooling if you don't have enough racks. If you are using baking parchment paper, you can just slide the entire sheet of cookies onto a suitable counter and leave them there until completely cooled, while you use the cookie sheet for the next batch of cookies.

✦ Shortbread ✦

MAKES 24 3-INCH COOKIES

A world-wide favorite and American by adoption since arriving here, undoubtedly in Colonial times. This recipe is as classic as it is delicious.

INGREDIENTS

> 8 ounces (2 sticks) salted butter, at room temperature
> 1/2 cup granulated sugar, plus additional for sprinkling
> 2 teaspoons vanilla
> 2 cups all-purpose flour

Premeasure and lay out all your ingredients on the counter.

PREPARE YOUR BAKING PAN

Use an *ungreased* cookie sheet.

PREHEAT THE OVEN

Set the oven to 350 degrees. Position the rack in the upper third of the oven. If you want to bake two trays of cookies at the same time, use the top and middle shelves of the oven and, midway through the baking, switch the trays and rotate them front to back at the same time.

MIXING THE DOUGH

1. In a bowl, using a mixer, cream the butter, sugar and vanilla at high speed for several minutes until the mixture is smooth and light.

2. Mix in the flour until the dough is uniform and smooth. If it is a little crumbly, just knead it with your fingers until it stays together in a smooth ball.
3. Deposit the dough on the cookie sheet by rounded teaspoonfuls in even rows, with a little space between. There should be very little spreading, if any. You can use a second spoon, or even your finger, to push the dough off the first spoon onto the cookie sheet. Have a glass of water handy in which to dip your spoons occasionally; this will make the depositing easier and faster.

Now pick up each cookie and roll it into a ball by gently rolling it between the palms of your hands. (If the dough is too soft to do this easily, refrigerate it for a short while.)

Place the balls on the cookie sheet and gently flatten each one with your wet fingers. Since there will be very little spreading, flatten them to their eventual serving size. Try to make each cookie the same thickness so they all get done at the same time. Prick the surface of each with a small fork and sprinkle some granulated sugar over the top.

BAKING THE COOKIES

Bake for 15 to 20 minutes or until the edges of the cookies just start to turn brown.

COOLING THE COOKIES

Let the cookies cool on the cookie sheet for a minute or two until they can be transferred easily to racks. They can also be placed on sheets of wax paper to finish cooling if you don't have enough racks. If you are using baking parchment paper, you can just slide the entire sheet of cookies onto a suitable counter and leave them there until completely cooled, while you use the cookie sheet for the next batch of cookies.

✦ Snickerdoodles ✦

MAKES 24 2½- INCH COOKIES

Another old New England favorite. How can anyone resist making a cookie with a name like Snickerdoodles? I couldn't resist and so I made them once and loved them. You will too, if you love the flavor of cinnamon. There's plenty of it (but not too much) both inside and out.

INGREDIENTS

For the Cookies

4 **ounces (1 stick) salted butter, at room temperature**
¾ **cup granulated sugar**
1 **teaspoon vanilla**
1 **large egg**
1½ **cups all-purpose flour**
1 **teaspoon cream of tartar**
½ **teaspoon baking soda**
1½ **teaspoons cinnamon**
¼ **teaspoon salt**

For Coating the Cookies

3 **teaspoons cinnamon**
3 **tablespoons granulated sugar**

Premeasure and lay out all your ingredients on the counter.

Prepare Your Baking Pan

Grease a cookie sheet lightly and evenly with solid shortening or cover it with a piece of baking parchment paper cut to fit.

Preheat the Oven

Set the oven to 375 degrees. Position the rack in the upper third of the oven. If you want to bake two trays of cookies at the same time, use the top and middle shelves of the oven and, midway through the baking, switch the trays and rotate them front to back at the same time.

Mixing the Dough

1. In a large bowl, using a mixer, beat the butter at high speed until it is soft and smooth, about 1 minute.
2. Add the sugar and vanilla and continue beating, at medium speed, until the mixture is light and fluffy.
3. At medium speed, add the egg, beating only until it is well blended. Remember to scrape down the bowl.
4. Blend together the flour, cream of tartar, baking soda, cinnamon, and salt. Then add to the butter and beat at medium speed until the mixture is uniform and smooth looking.
5. Deposit the dough on the cookie sheet by heaping teaspoonfuls in even rows, with space between to allow for spreading. You can use a second spoon, or even your finger, to push the dough off the first spoon onto the cookie sheet. Have a glass of water handy in which to dip your spoons occasionally; this will make the depositing easier and faster.

   Mix the cinnamon and sugar together and spread the mixture out on a plate. Then pick up each cookie and round it off neatly into a ball, dip it in the sugar-cinnamon mixture and replace it on the cookie sheet with the sugar-coated surface facing up.

6. Flatten each cookie with your wet fingers.

Baking the Cookies

Bake for 14 to 16 minutes until the tops of the cookies look set and start to turn brown.

Cooling the Cookies

Let the cookies cool on the cookie sheet for a minute or two until they can be transferred easily to racks. They can also be placed on sheets of wax paper to finish cooling if you don't have enough racks. If you are using baking parchment paper, you can just slide the entire sheet of cookies onto a suitable counter and leave them there until completely cooled, while you use the cookie sheet for the next batch of cookies.

✦ Sugar Cookies ✦

MAKES 24 2¹/₂-INCH COOKIES

Lots of butter, plenty of vanilla and just enough sugar make this pure and simple cookie a joy to eat. Although this is a drop cookie, it can also double as a "cut-out" cookie to make use of those cookie cutters that have been lying around unused in your drawer for so long. Either way you make them, they are a treat.

INGREDIENTS

6	ounces (1¹/₂ sticks) salted butter, at room temperature
³/₄	cup granulated sugar
2	teaspoons vanilla
1	large egg
1¹/₂	cups all-purpose flour
¹/₂	teaspoon baking powder
¹/₄	teaspoon mace or nutmeg
3	to 4 tablespoons granulated sugar

Premeasure and lay out all your ingredients on the counter.

PREPARE YOUR BAKING PAN

Grease a cookie sheet lightly and evenly with solid shortening or cover it with a piece of baking parchment paper cut to fit.

Preheat the Oven

Set the oven to 375 degrees. Position the rack in the upper third of the oven. If you want to bake two trays of cookies at the same time, use the top and middle shelves of the oven and, midway through the baking, switch the trays and rotate them front to back at the same time.

Mixing the Dough

1. In a large bowl, using a mixer, beat the butter at high speed until it is soft and smooth, about 1 minute.
2. Add the sugar and vanilla and continue beating at medium speed until the mixture is light and fluffy.
3. Add the egg, beating at medium speed just until it is well blended. Remember to scrape down the bowl.
4. Blend together the flour, baking powder and mace. Then add to the batter and mix at medium speed until the mixture is uniform and smooth looking.
5. Deposit the dough on the cookie sheet by heaping teaspoonfuls in even rows, with space between to allow for spreading. You can use a second spoon, or even your finger, to push the dough off the first spoon onto the cookie sheet. Have a glass of water handy in which to dip your spoons occasionally; this will make the depositing easier and faster.

    Spread the sugar out on a plate. Then pick up each cookie and round it off neatly into a ball, drop it in the sugar and replace it on the cookie sheet with the sugar-coated surface facing up.
6. Flatten each cookie fairly thin with your wet fingers.

To Make Cut-out Cookies

Divide the dough into two parts, flatten each one separately, wrap them in plastic and refrigerate for 30 to 40 minutes (or longer if you want to make the cookies later in the day, or even the next day). If you leave the dough in the refrigerator for long, it will need to become pliable at room temperature before you roll it out. When you are ready to make the cookies, just roll the dough flat on a floured surface, using a floured rolling pin, to a thickness of about $1/4$ inch and cut out the cookies with the cookie cutter or cutters you have chosen to use. Gently reroll the scraps of dough to make additional cookies. Bake as directed below.

Baking the Cookies

Bake for 14 to 17 minutes until the tops of the cookies look set and they are starting to turn brown around the edges.

Cooling the Cookies

Let the cookies cool on the cookie sheet for a minute or two until they are cooled just enough to be transferred easily to racks. They can also be placed on sheets of wax paper to finish cooling if you don't have enough racks. If you are using baking parchment paper, you can just slide the entire sheet of cookies onto a suitable counter and leave them there until completely cooled, while you use the cookie sheet for the next batch of cookies.

✦ Blondies ✦

MAKES 16 2-INCH SQUARES

A richly flavored bar with a butterscotch flavor instead of an intensely chocolaty one. Although many versions of blondies contain no chocolate at all, I have included chocolate chips because they make this blondie perfectly memorable. They will melt in your mouth, and many people prefer them to the conventional chocolate brownie. Almost unthinkable, isn't it?

INGREDIENTS

3/4	cup dark brown sugar, firmly packed
3	ounces (3/4 stick) salted butter, at room temperature
1	large egg
1	teaspoon vanilla
1	tablespoon water
1	cup all-purpose flour
1	teaspoon baking powder
1/4	teaspoon salt
1	cup (6 ounces) chocolate chips, semisweet
1/2	cup walnuts, in small pieces

Premeasure and lay out all your ingredients on the counter.

PREPARE YOUR BAKING PANS

Use an 8 × 8 × 2-inch square baking pan. Spray the inside of the pan with nonstick spray (PAM or something similar) or grease the pan with solid short-ening and dust with flour, tapping out the excess flour. It would also be helpful (but not essential) to cut out a piece of parchment or wax paper the size of the pan bottom and lay it in. It makes removing the cake from the pan a bit easier after baking and cooling.

PREHEAT THE OVEN

Set the oven to 350 degrees. Position the rack in the center of the oven.

MIXING THE BATTER

1. In a bowl, using a mixer, beat the sugar, butter, egg, vanilla and water until the mixture is smooth and light.
2. Thoroughly blend together the flour, baking powder and salt, add them to the mixing bowl and beat until they are just blended in.
3. Gently blend in the chocolate chips and walnuts. The dough will be stiff, which is all right.
4. Spread the dough evenly in the baking pan, using a spatula or your wet fingers.

BAKING THE BLONDIES

Bake for 25 to 35 minutes until golden brown and a toothpick or cake tester inserted in the center comes out clean, without any batter on it.

COOLING THE BLONDIES

After cooling for about 15 minutes in the pan, either turn the blondies out or let them cool in the pan and serve from there.

SERVING THE BLONDIES

Cut into 2-inch squares with a sharp knife.

✦ Brownies ✦

MAKES SIXTEEN 2-INCH SQUARES

I must have made at least fifty versions of chocolate brownies over the many years I have been baking and this, quite simply, is the best. The only way for you to find out whether this is true or not is to make it—following the recipe exactly. That includes beating the batter for the extra 2 minutes called for in the mixing directions.

INGREDIENTS

- 4 ounces (1 stick) salted butter, at room temperature
- 1¹/₂ cups granulated sugar
- 2 large eggs
- ¹/₂ cup plus 1 tablespoon unsweetened cocoa, sifted after measuring
- 1 cup plus 2 tablespoons all-purpose flour
- ¹/₂ teaspoon baking powder
- ¹/₄ teaspoon salt
- 1 tablespoon water
- 1 teaspoon vanilla
- ³/₄ cup walnuts, in small pieces

Premeasure and lay out all your ingredients on the counter.

PREPARE YOUR BAKING PAN

Use an 8-inch square baking pan. Spray the inside of the pan with nonstick spray (PAM or something similar) or grease the pan with solid shortening and dust with flour, tapping out the excess flour. It would also be helpful (but not essential) to cut out a piece of parchment or wax paper the size of the pan bottom and lay it in. It makes removing the brownies from the pan a bit easier.

PREHEAT THE OVEN

Set the oven to 350 degrees. Position the rack in the center of the oven.

MIXING THE BATTER

1. In a large bowl, using a mixer, beat the butter for a half minute or so, then add the sugar and beat until the mixture is well blended together.
2. Beat in the eggs.
3. Add the sifted cocoa and mix until the batter is smooth.
4. Thoroughly blend together the flour, baking powder and salt, add them to the mixing bowl and beat at medium speed *for 2 minutes.*
5. Add the water and vanilla and mix them in.
6. Gently blend in the walnuts. The dough will be stiff and sticky, which is all right.
7. Spread the dough evenly in the baking pan, using a spatula or your wet fingers.

BAKING THE BROWNIES

Bake for 30 to 40 minutes or until the top is set and a toothpick or cake tester inserted in the center comes out clean, without any batter on it.

COOLING THE BROWNIES

After cooling for about 15 minutes in the pan, either turn the brownies out or let them cool in the pan and serve from there. If you feel particularly decadent, spread the brownies with a Chocolate Glaze (see "Frostings and Glazes").

SERVING THE BROWNIES

Cut into 2-inch squares with a sharp knife.

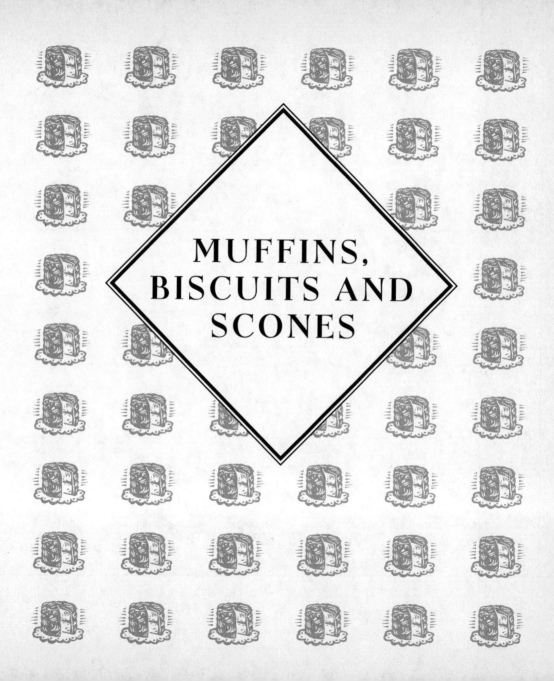

MUFFINS, BISCUITS AND SCONES

✦ Blueberry Muffins ✦

MAKES APPROXIMATELY 12 MUFFINS

Even if these muffins were made without blueberries, they would be perfectly delicious. With the additional burst of flavor coming from the blueberries, they are simply wonderful. Just be sure to use paper muffin cups when you make them.

INGREDIENTS

Use fresh blueberries if in season. If they are not in season, frozen may be used, but without syrup. Do not defrost before using.

1 to 1¹/₂ cups blueberries, fresh or frozen
2 tablespoons all-purpose flour

Dry Ingredients

2 cups all-purpose flour
¹/₂ teaspoon baking soda
2 teaspoons baking powder
¹/₂ teaspoon salt
¹/₄ teaspoon mace or nutmeg
1 cup granulated sugar, plus additional for sprinkling

Wet Ingredients

2 large eggs
6 tablespoons vegetable oil (corn or safflower)
1 cup sour cream

Gently toss the blueberries with the 2 tablespoons of flour and set aside.

Prepare Your Baking Pan

Put paper muffin liners into the cups of a standard-size muffin pan.

Preheat the Oven

Set the oven to 400 degrees. Position the rack in the center or lower third of the oven.

MIXING THE BATTER

1. Stir all the dry ingredients together thoroughly in a bowl.
2. In a separate bowl, combine the eggs, oil and sour cream.
3. Pour the egg–sour cream mixture over the dry ingredients and mix until the batter is uniform in appearance. Do not overmix.
4. Gently fold in the blueberries, using a large spatula or spoon.
5. Immediately fill the paper cups to the very top with the batter, using a large ice-cream scoop or large spoon.
6. Sprinkle a small amount of granulated sugar on the top of each muffin.

BAKING THE MUFFINS

Bake 20 to 25 minutes. Tops will be brown, the muffins will feel springy to the touch and a cake tester or toothpick will come out clean, without any batter on it.

COOLING THE MUFFINS

Cool in the muffin pan about 10 minutes and then take out the individual muffins and place them on racks to finish cooling.

✦ Bran Muffins ✦

MAKES 10 TO 12 MUFFINS

This is a special bran muffin recipe that will convert those people who steer away from healthful-sounding baked things on the theory that delicious taste is somehow sacrificed for the sake of healthfulness. In the case of these muffins, this couldn't be farther from the truth. Once tasted, these bran muffins will be a lifelong addition to your baking schedule. They are moist, fragrant, crunchy and absolutely delicious.

INGREDIENTS

Use natural, unprocessed bran in this recipe, *not* bran breakfast cereal.

Dry Ingredients

- 1⅓ cups all-purpose flour
- ¾ teaspoon baking powder
- ¾ teaspoon baking soda
- ½ cup granulated sugar
- ¼ teaspoon salt
- ½ cup walnut pieces
- ¾ cup chopped dates (or whole raisins rinsed in hot water)
- 1 cup wheat bran

Wet Ingredients

- **1 cup buttermilk**
- **1 large egg, slightly beaten**
- **6 tablespoons vegetable oil (canola or safflower)**
- **1 tablespoon molasses (preferably light)**
- **2 tablespoons water**

PREPARE YOUR BAKING PAN

Put paper muffin liners into the cups of a standard-size muffin pan or thoroughly grease the cups with a solid shortening. Grease a bit of the flat surface around the top of each cup to prevent any overflow of the muffins from sticking.

PREHEAT THE OVEN

Set the oven to 400 degrees. Position the rack in the center or lower third of the oven.

MIXING THE BATTER

1. Stir the dry ingredients together in a bowl.
2. Put the wet ingredients into a separate bowl and stir them all together.
3. Pour the wet ingredients over the dry ingredients and mix until everything is well incorporated and the batter is uniform in color and appearance. Do not overmix.
4. Fill the muffin cups seven-eighths full.

BAKING THE MUFFINS

Bake 20 to 22 minutes. Tops will be brown, the muffins will feel springy to the touch and a cake tester or toothpick inserted into the center will come out clean, without any batter on it.

COOLING THE MUFFINS

Cool the muffins in the muffin pan about 10 minutes and then take them out and place them on racks to finish cooling.

✦ Corn Muffins ✦

MAKES APPROXIMATELY 8 MUFFINS

If there was a three-way muffin race for popularity and the contestants were corn muffins, bran muffins and blueberry muffins, it would probably be corn muffins that would win. Not by much, but still the winner. I like corn muffins to taste like corn muffins and not like cake muffins with corn added, and this version does just that. I particularly like the little tang that the buttermilk gives them.

INGREDIENTS

Try to find stone-ground cornmeal (most health-food stores carry it). The degerminated cornmeal found in most supermarkets has less flavor.

Dry Ingredients

- 1 cup all-purpose flour
- 1 cup yellow cornmeal (stone-ground, if possible)
- 1½ teaspoons baking powder
- ½ teaspoon baking soda
- 4 tablespoons granulated sugar
- ¾ teaspoon salt

Wet Ingredients

- 1 large egg, slightly beaten
- 1 cup buttermilk
- ¼ cup milk
- ¼ cup vegetable oil (canola or safflower)

PREPARE YOUR BAKING PAN

Grease the cups of a standard-size muffin pan with solid shortening. Include a bit of the flat surface around the top of each cup to prevent any overflow of the muffin batter from sticking after it is baked. I usually put a very small dab of shortening into each cup with the point of a knife and then use a finger to thoroughly coat all the surface. This works better and is less messy than attempting to spray the surface with a nonstick cooking spray. I don't use paper liners with corn muffins because if you do, you give up the delicious taste of the crust.

PREHEAT THE OVEN

Set the oven to 400 degrees. Position the rack in the center or lower third of the oven.

MIXING THE BATTER

1. Stir the dry ingredients together thoroughly in a bowl.
2. Stir the wet ingredients together in a separate bowl.
3. Pour the wet ingredients over the dry ingredients and mix until the batter is uniform in appearance. Do not overmix.
4. Fill the muffin cups seven-eighths full.

BAKING THE MUFFINS

Bake 18 to 24 minutes. Tops will be brown, the muffins will feel springy to the touch and a cake tester or toothpick will come out clean, without any batter on it.

COOLING THE MUFFINS

Cool in the muffin pan about 10 minutes and then turn out the individual muffins and place them on racks to finish cooling.

SERVING THE MUFFINS

Corn muffins are at their best served slightly warm with butter and preserves available on the side.

✦ Buttermilk Biscuits ✦

MAKES 10 TO 12 BISCUITS

Bake them high and bake them tender and bake them with a crispy brown crust. Now you know most of the secrets of making delicious buttermilk biscuits. Another secret is to handle the easy-to-make dough gently and the last secret is to eat them warm from the oven. Now that you know all the secrets, here is the recipe to go with them. (P.S. Yes, they are also delicious refrigerated or frozen and then warmed in the oven, so make enough.)

INGREDIENTS

2　cups all-purpose flour
1/2　teaspoon salt
3　teaspoon baking powder
1/4　teaspoon baking soda
1　teaspoon sugar
3　ounces (3/4 stick) salted butter, cold
1　cup buttermilk

Note: If you have a craving for hot biscuits and you don't have buttermilk immediately available, you can certainly use milk or half-and-half or sweet cream and end up with perfectly delicious baking-powder biscuits. For me, the buttermilk adds that extra little tang and tenderness but there are many different schools and many different tastes and, no matter which way you go, you can't go wrong.

PREPARE YOUR BAKING PAN

Use an ungreased cookie sheet or a cookie sheet covered with baking parchment paper cut to fit.

PREHEAT THE OVEN

Set the oven to 450 degrees. Place the rack in the middle of the oven.

MIXING THE DOUGH BY HAND

1. Thoroughly blend together the flour, salt, baking powder, baking soda and sugar in a large bowl.
2. Cut the butter into several small pieces, add it to the flour and cut it into the flour with a pastry blender, or two knives, or your fingers until the mixture looks like coarse meal. Little bits of butter here and there are all right.
3. Add the buttermilk all at once and mix everything together with a large spoon or fork until a dough is formed. It will be sticky and not every bit of flour will have been incorporated but just go ahead and turn it all out on a floured surface.
4. Knead the dough quickly and gently, using both hands, for a very short time (30 to 40 seconds) until any excess flour has been incorporated and the dough sticks together as a soft, but still somewhat sticky, ball. Do not overmix or overknead the dough as it will result in less tender biscuits.
5. Roll out the dough with a rolling pin, or pat it down with the palms of your hands into a circle about $1/2$ inch thick.
6. Cut out the biscuits with a 2- or $2^{1}/_{2}$-inch biscuit cutter (or its equivalent in a wine or drinking glass) dipped in flour and be sure to use a straight up

and down cut without turning or twisting the cutter. Just resist that temptation to twist as you withdraw the cutter. Straight down and straight up is the way to go. Twisting causes lopsided biscuits.

7. Transfer the biscuits onto the cookie sheet with a spatula and leave a little space around each one.

8. Handling as little and as lightly as possible, follow the same procedure with the trimmings.

MIXING THE DOUGH IN THE FOOD PROCESSOR

Do steps 1, 2 and 3 in the food processor and the remaining by hand.

BAKING THE BISCUITS

Place the cookie sheet in the middle of the oven and bake until the biscuits are golden brown, 12 to 16 minutes.

SERVING THE BISCUITS

The biscuits are at their best when served hot or warm right from the oven, but they also freeze well and just require heating in a 350-degree oven until they are hot again.

✦ Popovers ✦

MAKES 7 LARGE POPOVERS

When you want a bit of excitement in the kitchen, all you have to do is make some popovers for breakfast. Just pour the thin, creamy batter into a well-greased muffin pan or popover pan, put the pan into a cold oven and then turn on the heat. Then it's time to take a shower or make the beds or read the paper or whatever. What comes out of the oven about 40 minutes later is eye opening—a hugely puffed-up golden shell with a hollow, eggy center and, yes, it tastes as good as it looks. Have preserves on the table, of course. One of the nice things about popovers is that you don't have to eat them all up at one time. They freeze beautifully and are still delicious when warmed up again on another day.

INGREDIENTS

> 3 tablespoons salted butter, melted
> 1 cup all-purpose flour
> 1/4 teaspoon salt
> 1 cup milk
> 2 large eggs

PREPARE YOUR BAKING PAN

Using a pastry brush, coat each cup of your baking pan liberally with 2 tablespoons of the melted butter.

The best popovers are made with special popover pans—either completely separated cups held together by metal rods or fairly large cups with tops that flare out a bit wider at the very top. However, they can certainly be made successfully with standard-size muffin pans, so don't hesitate to use yours. You can always buy the special pans if popovers become an important part of your cuisine. Incidentally, because we are starting in a cold oven, I would not recommend using those heavy cast-iron pans we usually associate with popovers, nor would I use heavy old-fashioned custard cups.

PREHEAT THE OVEN

Do *not* preheat your oven. Popovers started in a cold oven are so successful and so delicious and so much easier than the old method of preheating the baking pan.

MIXING THE BATTER BY HAND

Note: You can make the batter immediately before use or you can make it ahead of time and keep it in the refrigerator (even overnight).

1. Put the flour and salt in a mixing bowl (preferably one with a pouring lip), whisk them together and then add the milk, eggs and remaining table-spoon of melted butter and blend everything together until the batter is smooth. It will be a thin and pourable batter, which is the way that it should be.
2. If the bowl does not have a pouring lip, transfer the batter to a measuring cup for easier pouring.
3. Fill the well-buttered cavities in your baking pan two-thirds or three-quarters full.

MIXING THE BATTER IN A BLENDER

You can also make the batter by putting all the ingredients at once into your blender. Be sure, though, to put the liquid ingredients in first and then the flour and salt. Blend for about 10 seconds, remove the cover and scrape the sides down and then blend another 10 seconds or so until it is smooth. Do not get carried away and overblend.

BAKING THE POPOVERS

Put the popover pan into a cold oven and immediately turn the temperature up to 375 degrees. The baking time will be 40 to 45 minutes. *For the first half hour, don't dare to open the oven door to peek.* The popovers are done when they are high and golden brown in appearance and they feel dry and firm to the touch.

SERVING THE POPOVERS

Serve them hot, straight from the oven. Poke the tip of a sharp knife into the side of each popover to let some of the steam escape. This will help prevent sogginess. Leftover popovers may be frozen and then reheated in a 350-degree oven until they are hot enough to serve.

✦ Scones ✦

MAKES 8 SCONES

Before I included a recipe for scones in this all-American baking book, I asked myself whether an adopted child could be as loved and treasured as a natural one. The answer was, indeed, yes. And so here is the recipe for this nationally popular and universally loved rich and sweet biscuit. Although it is Scottish in origin, it is now American by adoption and it is one of the greatest gifts ever to the breakfast table or coffee or tea break. I use heavy cream in my recipe because it makes great scones.

INGREDIENTS

- 1³/₄ cups all-purpose flour
- 2¹/₂ teaspoons baking powder
- 2 tablespoons granulated sugar
- ¹/₂ teaspoon salt
- 2 ounces (¹/₂ stick) salted butter, chilled
- ¹/₃ cup heavy cream
- 2 large eggs
- ¹/₃ cup currants (or more if you prefer; raisins can be substituted)

PREPARE YOUR BAKING PAN

Use an *ungreased* cookie sheet.

PREHEAT THE OVEN

Set the oven to 425 degrees. Place the rack in the middle of the oven.

MIXING THE DOUGH BY HAND

1. Thoroughly blend the flour, baking powder, sugar and salt in a large bowl.
2. Cut the butter into several small pieces and then cut it into the flour with a pastry blender, or two knives, or your fingers until the mixture looks like coarse meal. Little bits of butter here and there are all right.
3. In a separate bowl, beat the cream and eggs together and reserve 2 tablespoons in a small cup. Add the rest to the dry ingredients all at once and mix everything together with a large spoon or fork until a dough is formed. It may be sticky and not every bit of flour may have been incorporated but just go ahead and turn it all out on a floured surface.
4. Add the currants to the dough and work them in with your hands as evenly as you can.
5. Knead the dough quickly and gently, using both hands, for as short a time as possible, until the dough sticks together as a soft but cohesive ball. Do not overmix or overknead the dough as it will result in less tender scones.
6. Roll out the dough with a rolling pin, or pat it down with the palms of your hands into a circle about ³/₄ inch thick.
7. Cut the scones into triangles. Just make believe that you are cutting a pie into eight equal portions. One complete stroke of the knife cuts the circle into two equal halves, another stroke gives you four equal quarters and the next two slices leave you with eight triangular scones.
8. Using a pastry brush, coat the top of each scone with the reserved egg and cream mixture and then sprinkle each with a little sugar.

9. Transfer the scones onto the cookie sheet with a spatula and leave a little space around each one.

MIXING THE DOUGH IN THE FOOD PROCESSOR

Do steps 1, 2 and 3 in the food processor and the remaining steps by hand.

BAKING THE SCONES

Place the cookie sheet in the middle of the oven and bake until the scones are golden brown, 14 to 16 minutes.

SERVING THE SCONES

The scones are at their best when served warm right from the oven, but they also freeze well and just require heating in a 350 degree oven.

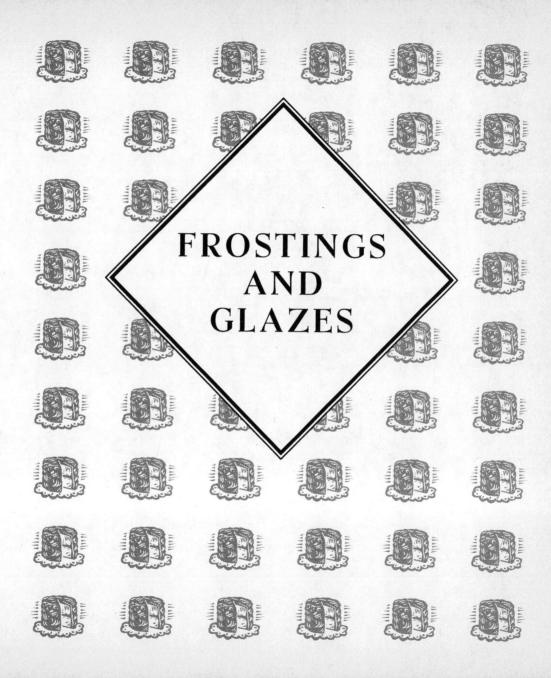

FROSTINGS
AND
GLAZES

Every single cake in this book is delicious on its own but, in practically every case, it can be transformed from "beautiful" to "spectacular" with just a very little effort.

The easiest decoration is to dust the cake with confectioners' sugar; all that is required is a powdered-sugar shaker with little round holes or wire mesh on top. A fine-meshed strainer could also serve in a pinch. Just put the cake on a large plate or board, dust it to the degree that looks right to you and then, using a large metal spatula, transfer it to a serving plate. All done in a minute or two and you'll certainly get a few extra "ooh's" and "ah's" from your guests. Also, there is nothing to prevent you from adding a dollop of sweetened whipped cream, a portion of poached fruit or a scoop of vanilla ice cream to each dish as it is served.

For those times when a little extra effort seems justified, I am including recipes for some very basic, but very delicious, frostings and icings. They can be prepared quickly and easily and they will certainly provide a magic touch to the cake's presentation. I have purposely kept the recipes simple and in no case will you need special equipment or a thermometer to measure the temperature of boiling syrups.

I have also avoided using unusual or weird flavors or flavor combinations. The choice of chocolate fudge, creamy vanilla, fresh orange, fresh lemon or fluffy meringue should satisfy the most demanding palate. As everywhere else in this book, my aim was to keep it simple but make it wonderful.

✦ Chocolate Fudge Frosting ✦

4 ounces unsweetened chocolate
4 ounces (1 stick) salted butter
1/2 cup milk
1 teaspoon vanilla
1 1-pound box confectioners' sugar (1 pound equals approximately 4 cups)

1. Melt the chocolate and butter by stirring them in the top of a double boiler over simmering water. Or put them in a microwave-safe bowl, cover it with wax paper or plastic wrap, put the bowl in the microwave and turn it on high for about 1 minute. Thereafter, check it every 30 seconds or so until the chocolate is mostly melted. Try to finish the melting by stirring the last few remaining small pieces of chocolate while it is away from the heat. Or, if you like to live dangerously and promise to be careful, you can put them both into a small heavy-bottomed saucepan and stir continuously over low heat until the chocolate is melted. But remember: Chocolate burns quickly!

2. When the chocolate/butter mixture is liquid, pour it into a mixing bowl, add all the other ingredients and beat steadily until the frosting is very smooth and creamy. At this point, it is warm and soft and perfect for pouring over a 13 × 9-inch cake.

3. As the frosting cools, it starts to set up and thicken. When it reaches a spreadable consistency, you can use it to frost a layer cake. If it has thickened a little too much to spread easily, just beat it again and this will soften it.

The above recipe will make a sufficient amount to generously fill and frost an 8-inch or 9-inch layer cake. Half the recipe will frost a dozen or so cupcakes.

You can preserve extra frosting for later use by covering it and putting it into the refrigerator or freezer. Just be sure to allow it to reach room temperature before use.

✦ Vanilla Frosting ✦

6 **tablespoons salted butter, at room temperature**
1 **1-pound box confectioners' sugar (1 pound equals approximately**
   4 cups)
¼ **cup milk (more may be required in the mixing)**
2 **teaspoons vanilla**

1. Place all the ingredients in a mixing bowl and beat until the frosting is soft, smooth and creamy. If necessary to make it easily spreadable, add additional milk, *but only 1 tablespoon at a time.* I usually find that I do not have to add the extra milk.

The above recipe will make a sufficient amount to generously fill and frost an 8-inch or 9-inch layer cake. A half recipe will also frost a dozen or so cupcakes.

You can save extra frosting for later use by wrapping it carefully and putting it into the refrigerator or freezer. Just be sure to allow it to reach room temperature before use.

✦ Fluffy Meringue Frosting ✦

This is a delightfully simple version of the classic Seven-Minute Frosting.

> 3/4 cup granulated sugar
> 2 tablespoons water
> 1/4 teaspoon cream of tartar
> 1/8 teaspoon salt
> 1/4 cup corn syrup
> 2 large egg whites
> 1 teaspoon vanilla

1. In a saucepan, mix together the sugar, water, cream of tartar, salt and corn syrup. Bring to a boil while stirring constantly. Remove from the heat and set aside.
2. Beat the egg whites with the vanilla until they are foamy. Continue beating at high speed as you pour the hot sugar mixture into the egg whites in a thin stream. Beat until the mixture forms very stiff and glossy peaks.

This frosting should be used on the same day it is mixed. If you like, you can also fold sweetened flaked or shredded coconut into the frosting or scatter it over the frosted cake.

The above recipe will make a sufficient amount to generously fill and frost an 8- or 9-inch layer cake.

✦ Fresh Lemon Frosting ✦

4 ounces (1 stick) salted butter, at room temperature
3 ounces cream cheese, at room temperature
1 1-pound box confectioners' sugar (1 pound equals approximately 4 cups)
2 tablespoons freshly squeezed lemon juice
1 teaspoon grated lemon rind
1 teaspoon vanilla

1. Beat the butter and cream cheese together until they are soft and creamy.
2. Add the other ingredients and beat until the frosting is soft, smooth and creamy. If it's necessary to make it easily spreadable, add a little milk or water *but only 1 tablespoon at a time*. If you taste it now and you think it needs a little more lemon kick, you can add some more lemon juice instead of the milk or water.

The above recipe will make a sufficient amount to generously fill and frost an 8- or 9-inch layer cake. A half recipe will also frost a dozen or so cupcakes.

You can save extra frosting for later use by covering it and putting it into the refrigerator or freezer. Just be sure to allow it to reach room temperature before use.

✦ Fresh Orange Frosting ✦

4 ounces (1 stick) salted butter, at room temperature
3 ounces cream cheese, at room temperature
1/4 cup freshly squeezed orange juice (more may be required in the
mixing)
2 teaspoons grated orange rind
1 1-pound box confectioners' sugar (1 pound equals approximately
4 cups)
1 teaspoon vanilla

1. Beat the butter and cream cheese together until they are soft and creamy.
2. Add the other ingredients and beat until the frosting is soft, smooth and
creamy. If necessary to make it easily spreadable, add additional orange
juice (or milk or water) *but only 1 tablespoon at a time.*

The above recipe will make a sufficient amount to generously fill and frost an
8-inch or 9-inch layer cake. A half recipe will also frost a dozen or so cupcakes.

You can save extra frosting for later use by covering it and putting it into
the refrigerator or freezer. Just be sure to allow it to reach room temperature
before use.

✦ Chocolate Glaze ✦

1   **cup water**
2   **ounces unsweetened chocolate**
2   **tablespoons salted butter**
2   **cups confectioners' sugar**
1   **teaspoon vanilla**

1. Boil about 1 cup of water and set it aside.
2. Melt the chocolate and butter by stirring them in the top of a double boiler over simmering water. Or put them in a microwave-safe bowl, cover it with wax paper, plastic wrap or a paper plate, put the bowl in the microwave and turn the microwave on high for about 1 minute. Thereafter, check it every 30 seconds or so until the chocolate is mostly melted. Try to finish the melting by stirring the last few remaining small pieces of chocolate while it is away from the heat. Or, if you like to live dangerously and promise to be careful, you can put them both into a small heavy-bottomed saucepan and stir continuously over low heat until the chocolate is melted. But remember: Chocolate burns quickly!

3. Pour the hot chocolate-butter mixture into a mixing bowl, add the confectioners' sugar and vanilla and start to mix them together. It will look dry and crumbly.

4. Add ¼ cup of boiling water while mixing steadily and the glaze should turn smooth, shiny and pourable. If necessary, add more hot water, but no more than 1 teaspoon at a time. Use immediately.

Pour over the cake to cover it. If possible, have the cake sitting on a metal cooling rack over a large plate so that the drippings may be saved. This glaze works particularly well with layer cakes and cakes baked in a Bundt pan. Let the glaze dry a bit and then transfer the cake to the serving dish with a large metal spatula.

This glaze is also great for dipping the top of cupcakes into and then turning them right side up to dry, and for spreading over the top of a pan of chocolate brownies.

✦ Vanilla Glaze (or Drizzle) ✦

This glaze is used primarily for drizzling over coffee cakes and cakes made in Bundt or tube pans.

1½ cups confectioners' sugar
1   teaspoon vanilla
3   tablespoons milk

1. Put all the ingredients into a small mixing bowl and, with a hand whisk, stir rapidly until the mixture is creamy and runny. It should be rather thick and heavy but still drop off a spoon in a slow-moving but steady stream. To achieve this, you may have to add a drop more of milk or a bit more of confectioners' sugar. Be sure to add the milk sparingly, a few drops at a time, as a very little goes a long way. You want the glaze to be heavy, not watery. I seldom find it necessary to add those extra few drops of milk.

2. Using a spoon, or even the whisk, simply drizzle the glaze over the cake in a random but decorative fashion.

✦ Orange or Lemon Glaze ✦

These glazes are variations of the Vanilla Glaze; just make the following substitutions.

Orange Glaze: Substitute 3 tablespoons of orange juice for the 3 tablespoons of milk in the preceeding recipe. For more orange flavor, add 1 or 2 teaspoons of grated orange peel.

Lemon Glaze: Substitute 1 tablespoon of lemon juice for 1 tablespoon of the milk in the preceding recipe. In other words, you'll be using 2 tablespoons of milk and 1 tablespoon of lemon juice. For more lemon flavor, add 1 or 2 teaspoons of grated lemon peel.

Index